GW01045354

B1
PRELIMINARY 1

WITH ANSWERS

AUTHENTIC PRACTICE TESTS

Cambridge University Press
www.cambridge.org/elt

Cambridge Assessment English
www.cambridgeenglish.org

Information on this title: www.cambridge.org/9781108676410

© Cambridge University Press and UCLES 2019

First published 2019

20 19 18 17 16 15 14 13 12 11 10 9 8 7 6 5 4 3 2

Printed in Italy by Rotolito S.p.A.

A catalogue record for this publication is available from the British Library

ISBN 978-1-108-67641-0 Preliminary 1 Student's Book with answers with Audio
ISBN 978-1-108-72368-8 Preliminary 1 Student's Book without answers
ISBN 978-1-108-72369-5 Audio CDs (2)

Contents

Introduction

This collection of four complete practice tests contains papers from the *Cambridge English Qualifications B1 Preliminary* examination. Students can practise these tests on their own or with the help of a teacher.

The *B1 Preliminary* examination is part of a series of Cambridge English Qualifications for general and higher education. This series consists of five qualifications that have similar characteristics but are designed for different levels of English language ability. The *B1 Preliminary* certificate is recognised around the world as proof of intermediate level English skills for industrial, administrative and service-based employment. It is also accepted by a wide range of educational institutions for study purposes.

Cambridge English Qualifications	CEFR Level	UK National Qualifications Framework Level
C2 Proficiency	C2	3
C1 Advanced	C1	2
B2 First	B2	1
B1 Preliminary	B1	Entry 3
A2 Key	A2	Entry 2

Further information

The information contained in this practice book is designed to be an overview of the exam. For a full description of all of the above exams, including information about task types, testing focus and preparation, please see the relevant handbooks which can be obtained from the Cambridge Assessment English website at: **cambridgeenglish.org**.

The structure of *B1 Preliminary*: an overview

The *Cambridge English Qualifications B1 Preliminary* examination consists of four papers:

Reading: 45 minutes
Candidates need to be able to understand the main points from signs, newspapers and magazines and use vocabulary and structures correctly.

Writing: 45 minutes
Candidates need to be able to respond to an email and to write either an article or a story.

Listening: 30 minutes approximately (plus 6 minutes to transfer answers)
Candidates need to show they can follow and understand a range of spoken materials including announcements and discussions about everyday life.

Speaking: 12–17 minutes
Candidates take the Speaking test with another candidate or in a group of three. They are tested on their ability to take part in different types of interaction: with the examiner, with the other candidate and by themselves.

	Overall length	Number of tasks/parts	Number of items
Reading	45 mins	6	32
Writing	45 mins	2	–
Listening	approx. 30 mins	4	25
Speaking	12–17 mins	4	–
Total	approx. 2 hours 12 mins		

Grading

All candidates receive a Statement of Results and candidates whose performance ranges between CEFR Levels A2 and B2 (Cambridge English Scale scores of 120–170) also receive a certificate.

- Candidates who achieve **Grade A** (Cambridge English Scale scores of 160–170) receive the Preliminary English Test certificate stating that they demonstrated ability at Level B2.

- Candidates who achieve **Grade B** or **C** (Cambridge English Scale scores of 140–159) receive the Preliminary English Test certificate at Level B1.

- Candidates whose performance is below A2 level, but falls within **Level A2** (Cambridge English Scale scores of 120–139), receive a Cambridge English certificate stating that they have demonstrated ability at Level A2.

For further information on grading and results, go to the website (see page 5 for details).

Speaking: an overview for candidates

The Speaking test lasts 12–17 minutes. You will take the test with another candidate. There are two examiners but only one of them will talk to you. The examiner will ask you questions and ask you to talk to the other candidate.

Part 1 (2–3 minutes)
The examiner will ask you and your partner some questions in turn. These questions will be about your personal details, daily routines, likes, dislikes, etc. You will only speak to the examiner in this part.

Part 2 (2–3 minutes)
The examiner will give you a colour photograph to talk about. The photograph will show an everyday situation. You will be given one minute to describe what you can see in the photograph.

Part 3 (3 minutes)
In this part, you and your partner will talk to each other. The examiner will give you a card with some illustrations on it that are connected to an imaginary situation. You will then be given about two minutes to discuss ideas with your partner. During the discussion, you should make and respond to suggestions, discuss alternatives, make recommendations and negotiate agreement with your partner.

Part 4 (3–4 minutes)
The examiner will ask you and your partner some questions about the topic introduced in Part 3. The questions will focus on your likes, dislikes, habits and opinions. The examiner will either ask you to respond individually to the questions, or to discuss them with your partner.

Test 1

READING (45 minutes)

Part 1

Questions 1–5

For each question, choose the correct answer.

1

College Shop
Now is the time to buy
essential items like pens and
folders – prices reduced
until Friday.
Open daily during lunch
breaks. Also for 30 minutes
after last class everyday
apart from Monday.

A Students must go to the college shop to buy certain items for their studies.

B Students can take advantage of special offers at the college shop at the moment.

C Students may visit the college shop at lunchtime every day except Monday.

2

Hi Max
I'm afraid I'll no longer
be able to come on
the shopping trip
tomorrow. My aunt is
visiting and didn't give
us much notice.
Jake

Jake is writing to

A suggest a new date for a shopping trip.

B invite Max to meet one of his relatives.

C cancel an arrangement he had made.

3

Special Offer

Order any pizza by
7 p.m. and
get another
one half-price!

A All the pizzas in the restaurant are included in this offer.

B Any pizza ordered before 7 p.m. costs less than the usual price.

C At certain times, a customer can get two pizzas for the price of one.

4

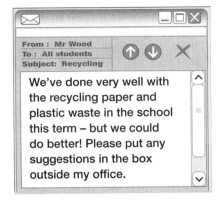

From : Mr Wood
To : All students
Subject: Recycling

We've done very well with the recycling paper and plastic waste in the school this term – but we could do better! Please put any suggestions in the box outside my office.

A Mr Wood has made suggestions on how to recycle waste produced by the school.

B Recycling materials should be put into the box outside Mr Wood's office.

C Mr Wood wants new ideas on ways to improve waste recycling in the school.

5

Hi Sam,
Thanks for taking me to the cinema last night. I didn't say at the time but I was a bit frightened! I think I need to watch a comedy next time!
Mel

Mel is texting to

A accept Sam's invitation to the cinema.

B admit to Sam that she found the film scary.

C ask when Sam can see another film with her.

Part 2

Questions 6–10

For each question, choose the correct answer.

The people below all want to find a book to read.
On the opposite page there are eight book reviews.
Decide which book would be the most suitable for the people below.

biography
— autobiography

G

6

Ahmed enjoys reading about real people, especially if they tell their own story. He'd like to read a book by someone who's had to deal with difficulties in their life.

(

7

Pritti loves doing all kinds of sport. She'd like to learn as much as possible about top sportspeople from all over the world and how they've managed to achieve their goals.

E

8

Conal loves nature and enjoys writing about it. He wants ideas to help him further develop his writing skills and would love to have a career as a writer.

B

9

Elif likes reading books about adventures. She loves learning about people who did brave things in the past, and how their actions have influenced the way we live today.

H

10

Stefan enjoys travelling and is keen to discover more about other cultures. He also wants to learn how to make typical dishes from a variety of countries.

Book reviews

A Being Me
This book is full of practical advice for anyone who wants to be fit and healthy. Famous sportspeople have contributed their favourite recipes, and you'll also find instructions for a daily exercise routine.

B Endless Days
In this book, the novelist tells the true story of the first pilots to fly across the Atlantic. With plenty of photographs and a detailed discussion of the importance of these events for the modern world, the book successfully brings history to life for readers everywhere.

C Action Plan
Action Plan is all about famous athletes, and there are some amazing photos of them competing. There are also lots of interviews about what they've done to succeed in their careers. You'll find out about things like the food they eat, the number of hours they train, and what they do to prepare for important competitions.

D Memories
The prize-winning author of *Memories* is famous for his unusual writing style and exciting adventure stories. In this book, he takes us on a journey around the world and teaches us a lot about other cultures and their histories. He describes some of the world's most beautiful nature, as well as the many interesting people he has met.

E Days in the Sun
In this book, a well-known author describes his happy early life growing up on a small Irish farm and how travelling around the countryside inspired him to become an author. He describes in detail how he improved his style, and his experiences will interest anyone who is hoping to get their own work published.

F Parrots in Paradise
This newly published adventure story is about a young girl who's lost on a beautiful island with only birds and animals for company. The story deals with some of the difficulties she has, but there's also lots of excitement. If you love well-written fiction, this book's for you!

G Night Light
In *Night Light*, the writer tells us how he became a world-class athlete. He talks about his life as a blind person, and describes the challenges he faced on his way to the top in the world of sports. The book is written in an entertaining and amusing style, which makes it a very enjoyable read.

H Our Lives
This is the perfect book if you're interested in how people live in different parts of the world. It also includes recipes for traditional meals from these places. There are wonderful photos, not only of the people, but also of the wildlife and scenery in each location.

Part 3

Questions 11–15

For each question, choose the correct answer.

Cyclist Vicky Harmiston

Reporter Mark Lewis writes about Vicky Harmiston, who has had a successful career as a track cyclist – a cyclist who races on special race tracks.

When Vicky Harmiston was a child, her parents gave her and her brother Jamie the freedom to decide what they did in their spare time. Vicky chose to do lots of different sports. She was a good swimmer, and the coach at the swimming club she went to thought she might be good enough to become a champion. But the club was a long way from her home so it was difficult for her to fit in the training around her schoolwork. When they were teenagers, Jamie, who loved cycling, bought himself a special track-racing bike and started taking part in competitions. Vicky thought it looked very exciting and decided to try it for herself. She says that was the best decision she ever made. Soon she was cycling every day and doing really well. The track was near her school, which meant it was no problem for her to attend training sessions after school every day.

Vicky went on to have a successful career in track cycling and won several competitions. Then, when she was 28, she retired from competitive cycling. Vicky told me: 'For years I'd loved winning competitions but I began to get a bit tired of the whole thing – and when the excitement stops, there's no point. Luckily, I went on to have a new career.'

Vicky got a job with a charity called CycleZone. 'We work with young people who have never enjoyed sport,' she says. 'The first thing we do is teach them to ride a bike. We want them to learn to believe in themselves and their own abilities. CycleZone does a great job, and it gets young people together so they're part of a wider group.'

The charity uses celebrities to advertise the work they do. Vicky says, 'I know some people aren't sure whether the support of a celebrity is always positive for a charity. They say the celebrities are only doing it to push themselves forward, which prevents the public from seeing the real work of the charity. But if famous singers and actors, for example, can help, I think they should.'

11   When Vicky first started cycling

    A   she had a very good coach.

    B   her parents gave her helpful advice.

    C   she could get to a race track easily.

    D   her brother gave her a great bike.

12   Why does Vicky say she stopped cycle racing?

    A   She felt she was too old to do it.

    B   She was becoming bored with it.

    C   She had won everything she wanted.

    D   She was preparing for a new career.

13   What does the charity CycleZone do for young people?

    A   It teaches them how to do track racing.

    B   It supports those who have talent.

    C   It offers them the chance to try a variety of sports.

    D   It helps them become more confident.

14   According to Vicky, some people believe that celebrities can

    A   take attention away from what a charity does.

    B   help people understand a charity's work.

    C   make the public care less about a charity.

    D   encourage more people to become involved with a charity.

15   What would Vicky say on her blog?

    A

> As a child, I always knew what I wanted to do when I grew up. But I never expected to become so famous.

    B

> If you join CycleZone, you'll get to meet celebrities and learn how they've become successful.

    C

> Although track cycling is not the only sport I've been good at, I've never regretted my choice of career.

    D

> In my spare time I love going to schools and helping groups of children learn to ride bikes.

Part 4

Questions 16–20

Five sentences have been removed from the text below.
For each question, choose the correct answer.
There are three extra sentences which you do not need to use.

At home together

Taimi Taskinen is an 83-year-old woman who lives in a care home called Rudolf House in Helsinki, Finland. A care home is a place where old people can live and be looked after if they don't live with their families. At Rudolf House, there are lots of stairs, so there are some rooms which elderly people can't access easily. As a result, the city council decided to rent these spare rooms to young people. They called this new housing programme 'The House that Fits'.

When Taimi heard about the council's plan, she wondered how it was going to work. **16** [   ] She couldn't imagine what she'd have in common with young people who weren't family members. Then, one morning a few days later, a young man appeared outside her room. **17** [   ]

'Hi! I'm your new neighbour,' the young man said. 'My name's Jonatan Shaya. Mind if I come in?' 'Please do,' she replied, immediately curious. 'I'll make coffee,' he announced, going into her tiny kitchen. 'Why don't you tell me about yourself?' he asked, as he brought their drinks to the table.

18 [   ] She also told him about her family and how much she loved making art.

In turn, 20-year-old Jonatan told Taimi he'd been living in Helsinki with his mother and younger brother until they moved away. He was in the middle of a course in the city, training to become a chef. **19** [   ] That's when he heard about 'The House that Fits' on social media. The council's post resulted in over 300 young people applying to live at Rudolf House. They had face-to-face interviews and wrote short essays about why they wanted to live there. **20** [   ] And that's how the unlikely friendship between Taimi and Jonatan began.

A   Surprising herself, she talked about growing up in a lakeside town in eastern Finland.

B   Therefore, he needed to find somewhere to live.

C   As a result, she wasn't sure whether the young people had arrived.

D   She'd left the door open, as she always did in the morning.

E   In the end, three of them, including Jonatan, were chosen.

F   Because of this, Jonatan has to be a good neighbour and spend 30 hours a month with Taimi.

G   It would be the first time that anything like this had happened at Rudolf House.

H   Instead, they just talked, as if they'd known each other forever.

Part 5

Questions 21–26

For each question, choose the correct answer.

The invention of crisps

Potato crisps were invented by accident in 1853, by a chef called George Crum. He was extremely **(21)** .... of his cookery skills, and the expensive hotel where he worked attracted customers who were **(22)** .... to eating only the best food.

One evening, a particularly difficult-to-please guest complained about Crum's fried potatoes. 'They're too thick,' he said, 'too soft, and have no flavour.' He **(23)** .... that they should be replaced.

The customer's negative **(24)** .... made Crum extremely angry, so he decided to annoy the customer. He cut a potato into paper-thin slices, fried the pieces until they were hard, then put far too much salt on them. 'He'll hate them,' Crum thought. But the customer loved them and ordered more.

News of this new snack travelled fast and an absolutely **(25)** .... global industry has grown from Crum's invention – even though his fried potatoes were actually **(26)** .... to taste disgusting!

21	**A** proud	**B** satisfied	**C** pleased	**D** impressed
22	**A** prepared	**B** familiar	**C** used	**D** known
23	**A** convinced	**B** wanted	**C** needed	**D** demanded
24	**A** comments	**B** notes	**C** reasons	**D** explanations
25	**A** big	**B** huge	**C** large	**D** wide
26	**A** hoped	**B** intended	**C** attempted	**D** tried

Part 6

Questions 27–32

For each question, write the correct answer.
Write **one** word for each gap.

Moving house

Hi Alex,

How are you? This week's been a very busy one for me – I finally moved house!
(27) .... wasn't until I started to pack a few days ago that I realised how
much stuff I had. I really think moving house is one of the **(28)** .... stressful
things I've ever done! I was sad to leave my old house – after **(29)** ...., I'd
lived there my whole life so I have lots of good memories.

Anyway, I'm looking **(30)** .... to being in this new house. It's not as big as the
old one, but **(31)** .... least it's got a great garden. I'm planning to have
a small party on Saturday night. Are you free then? Why don't you come along
(32) .... you are? I hope you can make it. Let me know.

All the best,

Sam

WRITING (45 minutes)

Part 1

You **must** answer this question.
Write your answer in about **100 words** on the answer sheet.

Question 1

Read this email from your English-speaking college classmate Alex and the notes you have made.

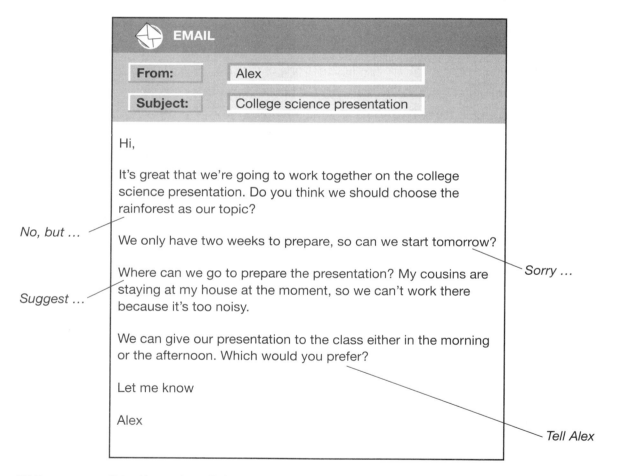

EMAIL

From: Alex

Subject: College science presentation

Hi,

It's great that we're going to work together on the college science presentation. Do you think we should choose the rainforest as our topic?

No, but …

We only have two weeks to prepare, so can we start tomorrow?

Sorry …

Where can we go to prepare the presentation? My cousins are staying at my house at the moment, so we can't work there because it's too noisy.

Suggest …

We can give our presentation to the class either in the morning or the afternoon. Which would you prefer?

Let me know

Alex

Tell Alex

Write your **email** to Alex using **all the notes**.

Part 2

Choose **one** of these questions.
Write your answer in about **100 words** on the answer sheet.

Question 2

You see this announcement in an English-language magazine.

Articles wanted!

Is shopping boring?

What do you like and dislike about shopping?
What could shopping centres do to attract more people?

Write us an article answering these questions. The best one will win a prize!

Write your **article**.

Question 3

Your English teacher has asked you to write a story.
Your story must begin with this sentence.

Jack climbed out of the boat and ran as fast as he could to the beach.

Write your **story**.

LISTENING (approximately 30 minutes)

Part 1

Questions 1–7

For each question, choose the correct answer.

---

1 Where does the man think he left his wallet?

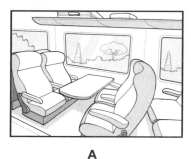

A

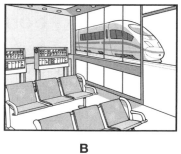

B

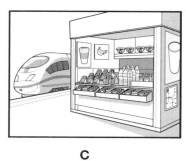

C

2 What is tomorrow's talk at the Nature Society about?

A

B

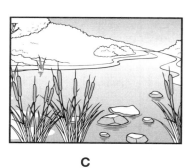

C

3 What will the woman order for lunch?

A

B

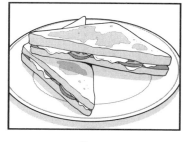

C

4   How did the woman find out about the exhibition?

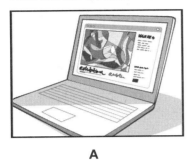

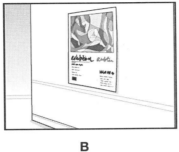

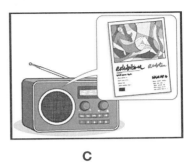

A   B   C

5   What is the woman's brother doing?

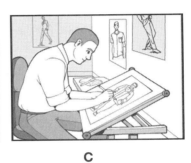

A   B   C

6   How will the woman travel to her meeting?

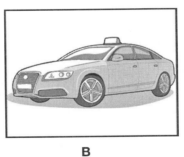

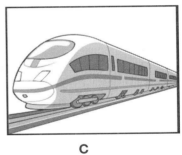

A   B   C

7   Which sport has the man stopped doing?

A   B   C

Part 2

Questions 8–13

For each question, choose the correct answer.

---

8 You will hear two people talking about buying a bicycle.
The woman suggests that the man should

    A   try looking online.

    B   go to a different shop.

    C   get advice from an expert.

9 You will hear a man telling his friend about his Welsh language course.
What does the man say about it?

    A   The teacher speaks too fast.

    B   The lessons are too long.

    C   The grammar is too difficult.

10 You will hear a woman telling her colleague about her weekend.
What did the woman like about it?

    A   visiting a new place in the city

    B   seeing her children enjoying themselves

    C   having a chance to relax

11 You will hear two friends talking about a new restaurant.
They both think the restaurant would be better if

    A   the food was fresher.

    B   the service was faster.

    C   the prices were cheaper.

12 You will hear two old friends talking at a party.
How is the man's appearance different from before?

    A   He has grown a beard.

    B   He has started wearing glasses.

    C   He has changed his style of clothes.

13 You will hear two colleagues talking about a meeting.
How does the woman feel about it?

    A   annoyed that she will have to attend it

    B   worried that her presentation will be unpopular

    C   surprised that it is still going to take place

Part 3

Questions 14–19

For each question, write the correct answer in the gap.
Write **one** or **two words** or a **number** or a **date** or a **time**.

You will hear a man giving information to people who are starting a one-week singing course.

One-week singing course

Teachers

Jazz: Robert Park

Songs from musicals: **(14)** Susan ....

Concert

When: Friday, at **(15)** .... p.m.

Colour of clothes: **(16)** ....

Other general information

Map of building: available from the **(17)** ....

Lunch: eat in the **(18)** ....

Car park: costs £ **(19)** .... per day

Part 4

Questions 20–25

For each question, choose the correct answer.

You will hear an interview with a man called Mickey Diaz, who is talking about his work as a hairdresser.

20 Why did Mickey decide to become a hairdresser?

    A He was offered a job by a friend.

    B He wanted to do what his family did.

    C He hoped to meet some famous people.

21 On a typical day at work, Mickey says that he

    A doesn't take enough time for breaks.

    B works longer hours than he would like to.

    C tries to do a range of jobs.

22 The part of the job which Mickey likes most is

    A creating new haircuts.

    B hearing about customers' lives.

    C using his imagination.

23 What part of his job does Mickey dislike?

    A having to do boring courses

    B sharing ideas with colleagues

    C dealing with difficult customers

24 How does Mickey feel after cutting a customer's hair?

    A worried that the customer may be annoyed.

    B proud of what he's achieved.

    C keen to continue learning.

25 Mickey recommends that people who want to work as hairdressers

    A shouldn't take the first job they're offered.

    B shouldn't believe they know everything.

    C shouldn't expect to earn much at first.

Test 2

READING (45 minutes)

Part 1

Questions 1–5

For each question, choose the correct answer.

1

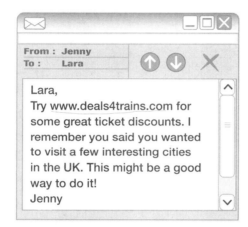

Jenny is emailing to

A suggest how Lara could do some sightseeing.

B remind Lara that she needs to book some cheap train tickets.

C invite Lara to visit some different places around the UK with her.

2

A People will be asked to discuss their favourite childhood sweets at the lecture.

B The lecture will be about how sweet shops have changed over the last century.

C The lecture will cover some surprising facts about sweets.

3

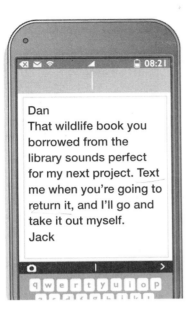

Dan
That wildlife book you borrowed from the library sounds perfect for my next project. Text me when you're going to return it, and I'll go and take it out myself.
Jack

A Jack is asking Dan's opinion about whether a book is suitable for his project.

B Jack wants Dan to let him know when a library book will be available.

C Jack is recommending to Dan a useful library book he has recently borrowed.

4

Tomato sauce
Store in cool, dry place. After opening, keep in fridge and use within six weeks, and not after date shown.

A Eat the sauce a maximum of six weeks after you start using it.

B Put the sauce in your refrigerator as soon as you bring it home.

C Make a note of the date when you bought the sauce.

5

DRUM TUTOR

All abilities & styles covered

Adults only (18+)

First lesson costs absolutely nothing when signing up for two months!

A The teacher is offering lessons to anyone interested in trying the drums.

B You must intend to study for a certain period to have the free session.

C To attend these classes, students must already be at a certain level.

Part 2

Questions 6–10

For each question, choose the correct answer.

The young people below are all interested in protecting the environment.
On the opposite page there are descriptions of eight websites on the environment.
Decide which website would be the most suitable for the people below.

B **6**

Ethan wants to know about environmental organisations around the world. He's interested in doing a project at home on energy production, and wants recommendations for other websites with up-to-date information on new research.

E **7**

Mario is interested in how the way he gets to work affects the environment, and wants ideas to reduce any negative effects. He'd like to meet local people who share his interest in the environment.

F **8**

Sylvia is keen to know what she can do with items she doesn't need, rather than throw them away. She'd like the opportunity to ask environmental experts about their work.

C **9**

Declan wants to know where to find clothes produced without damaging the environment. He'd like to learn about recycling processes, and see how recycling is done internationally.

H **10**

Tasha wants to help her family save energy, and get a basic introduction to studying the environment for a college project. She'd also like to buy something created from recycled items.

Websites on the environment

A **futurenow.org**
Find answers here about how much energy is used around the planet. And if you're planning a journey, put in your route to compare the energy used by different types of transport, and choose the one that's best for the environment.

B **ourworld.org**
This site lists the best places online to learn the latest results of scientific studies on issues affecting the environment. Or if you prefer working things out for yourself, there are experiments to do like making your own power using sunlight! You'll also find information on groups all over the planet working to protect the environment.

C **cleanplanet.org**
Discover how waste plastic, glass and metal are turned into new products, and watch clips showing different methods used around the world. There's also a section about how much attention various fashion companies pay to their effect on the environment. Use it to keep up with new trends!

D **globaleco.org**
This site explores the importance of energy in our daily lives, and also different ways of generating it without using oil or gas, for example by using wind power instead. There are links to UK companies that use these renewable energies, so you can find out more about what they do.

E **eco.org**
Contact others who also care about environmental issues and find information about international groups; search for one to join in your area. You can also find out if your choice of transport damages the planet. If so, try the easy changes to your routine suggested here.

F **planetmatters.org**
Learn about what top scientists involved in research to protect our planet do day to day, as well as about their latest discoveries. There's a message board so you can post questions to them – you'll always get a quick reply. There's also a recycling section – find different uses for things that you might otherwise put in the bin.

G **worldaware.org**
Most people want to know what they can do to help protect our world. This site has everything you need to know about recycling: why it's important around the world, and how to get rid of items safely in your local area without harming the environment.

H **oneworld.org**
There's lots of environmental information here, whether you're just starting to explore the subject, or wanting to find out about the latest research. Gifts are on sale, too, made from objects and materials that are often thrown out – treat yourself and help the planet! There's also a useful guide on using less electricity at home – reduce those bills!

Part 3

Questions 11–15

For each question, choose the correct answer.

Basketball player

Luka Horvat writes about his early career.

My dad was a professional basketball player in Germany, as his father had been before him, and I went to watch many of his games when I was a kid. You might think that seeing so many matches would give me a love of the sport, but it actually had the opposite effect. I loved telling my friends how good my dad was, of course, especially when he won a game, but I used to take a book with me to read instead of watching.

Starting secondary school, I was still two years away from being a teenager but was already two metres tall. Seeing my height, my sports teacher asked if I'd be interested in training with the basketball team. Even though I enjoyed the session, I thought I'd need to develop my skills before I took part in a real match, but the teacher had more confidence in me than I did. It took me a while to agree, but a few weeks later I found myself playing against a team from another school. Mum and Dad coming to watch didn't really help – it made me more nervous. But it was OK in the end!

For the next four years, I practised every day and did really well, even joining an adult team before I moved abroad to a special sports academy in the USA when I was fifteen. The coach there trains Olympic basketball players, and it was fantastic to work with him. However, I can't say I enjoyed my first experience of living far from my parents. At home, I'd never been able to spend much time with my friends due to all the training, so that wasn't such a change for me. I got used to everything about my new life in the end, though, and my English improved quickly too!

I turned professional at the age of eighteen, three years after arriving in the USA. I'd been taller than most players in the professional league since I was fifteen, but had been much too light for my height, so had to get that right first. My coach already knew a team that would take me while I was still at college, so I joined them and have never regretted it.

---

11   What does Luka say about his childhood?

    A   He had a great interest in basketball.

    B   He enjoyed watching his father play basketball.

    C   He felt proud of his father's success at basketball.

    D   He knew he wanted to become a basketball player.

12   How did Luka feel before his first match at secondary school?

    A   He wasn't sure that he would do well.

    B   He was pleased that his parents would be there.

    C   He wasn't happy about his teacher's attitude.

    D   He was delighted to be part of the team.

13   Luka thinks the most difficult thing about moving to the USA was

    A   learning a new language.

    B   being away from his family.

    C   getting a good coach.

    D   missing his friends.

14   What did Luka have to do before he became a professional player?

    A   complete his studies

    B   find a suitable team

    C   reach a certain height

    D   put on weight

15   What would be a good way to introduce this article?

A
> Luka Horvat has always been as interested in reading as in basketball. Here, in his own words, he explains why.

B
> Luka Horvat tells us how he became the latest member of a sporting family to become a professional basketball player.

C
> Professional basketball player Luka Horvat explains how luck has been so much more important than hard work in his career.

D
> Even though he only started playing basketball as a teenager, Luka Horvat still managed to become a professional by the age of eighteen.

31

Part 4

Questions 16–20

Five sentences have been removed from the text below.
For each question, choose the correct answer.
There are three extra sentences which you do not need to use.

Adventures in the air

The first ever balloon flight carrying passengers was made by the Montgolfier brothers in 1783. They used hot air to float the balloon over 1,000 metres up into the sky. Nowadays, people still fly in hot-air balloons but there is also a less well-known sport called 'cluster ballooning'; instead of one big balloon, hundreds of small balloons are used.

Cluster ballooning was invented by a lorry driver called Larry Walters. Larry had wanted to fly using balloons for a long time. **16** | C | It took almost 20 years, however, for his dream to finally come true. One day, Larry decided to do an experiment: he wanted to try flying a few metres above his garden. So he bought 45 balloons, filled them with a gas called helium, and tied them to a chair. He then cut the rope that was holding the chair to the ground. **17** | F | The chair, with Larry sitting in it, floated several kilometres into the sky rather than just a few metres!

The wind was blowing strongly and Larry began to float out towards the sea. Things were getting dangerous. Then, to make matters even worse, the wind changed, and the balloons started to blow towards the local airport. Larry felt very worried. **18** | D | The story of Larry's flight was all over the news and this is how the adventure sport of cluster ballooning was born.

One experienced cluster balloonist, Leo Burns, flew his cluster balloons over the largest range of mountains in Europe – the Alps. This wasn't his first flight, though. Leo had got his pilot's licence several years before, so was already used to flying. **19** | G | According to Leo, there is no better way to fly. 'Cluster ballooning's amazing,' he says. 'The balloons are usually completely silent. **20** | B | They weren't as safe as modern cluster balloons either.'

A	He knew this would still make him feel very afraid.
B	The old-fashioned hot-air balloons made a horrible noise.
C	In fact, he was just a boy when he first started thinking about it.
D	Luckily, he landed safely after a couple of hours.
E	They are also much less dangerous.
F	However, there was an unexpected problem.
G	But these days, he prefers to use balloons.
H	Immediately after that, he tried to learn how this would be possible.

Part 5

Questions 21–26

For each question, choose the correct answer.

Whale songs

Did you know that a kind of whale, called a humpback whale, sings? In the 1960s it was
(21) ....C............ that humpbacks communicate with each other by making beautiful
noises. A record was **(22)** ....D............ in 1970 called *Songs of the humpback whale*,
which sold millions of copies. People were absolutely amazed to learn that some whales in
the deep oceans were so intelligent: in **(23)** ....A............ centuries people had thought
that whales had simple brains, like fish.

The songs of the whales were so popular that they were **(24)** ....B............ in recordings
of sounds from our planet which were **(25)** ....A............ into space in 1977. The
recordings were chosen to show the wide **(26)** ....D............ of life on our planet. People
hoped that, in the future, they might be found by intelligent creatures far out in space.

21	**A** explored	**B** invented	**C** discovered	**D** informed
22	**A** appeared	**B** delivered	**C** achieved	**D** produced
23	**A** previous	**B** old	**C** early	**D** ancient
24	**A** contained	**B** included	**C** consisted	**D** involved
25	**A** sent	**B** added	**C** kept	**D** placed
26	**A** sort	**B** difference	**C** kind	**D** variety

Part 6

Questions 27–32

For each question, write the correct answer.
Write **one** word for each gap.

My travel blog

This summer, I travelled to Copenhagen, the capital of Denmark, on my own. I am only
20 and to **(27)** ....be.......... honest, I was nervous about exploring a new city alone.
I decided to go on a free walking tour the first day I was there. I hoped the tour would help
me to become more familiar **(28)** ......with........ the city.

Unfortunately, the weather wasn't great, but the tour was still absolutely fantastic! Magnus,
our tour guide, knew all about the city's history. We also learnt loads **(29)** ....of............
interesting facts about Danish culture. At the end of the tour, he gave **(30)** ......us............
all suggestions for the best places **(31)** ....to.......... eat and visit.

Apart from learning so much, I actually had a lot more fun on the walking tour
(32) ......than............ I'd expected. It was an excellent way to experience the city, and
learn about its culture and history.

WRITING (45 minutes)

Part 1

You **must** answer this question.
Write your answer in about **100 words** on the answer sheet.

Question 1

Read this email from your English-speaking friend Robbie and the notes you have made.

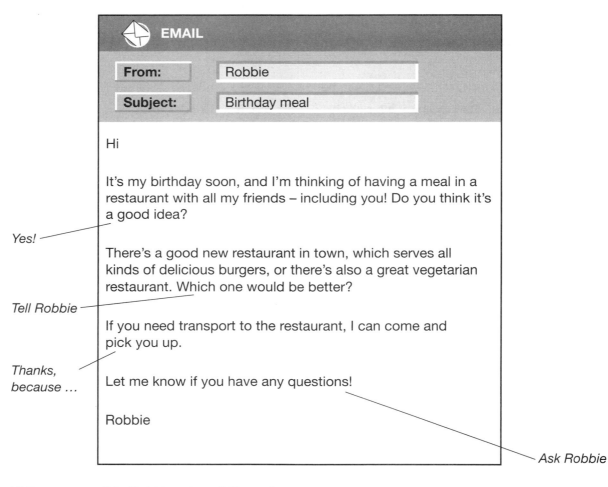

Write your **email** to Robbie using **all the notes**.

Part 2

Choose **one** of these questions.
Write your answer in about **100 words** on the answer sheet.

Question 2

You see this announcement on an English-language website.

> **Articles wanted!**
>
> # Free-time activities
>
> What activities can people your age do in their free time where you live?
> Do you enjoy taking part in organised activities? Why?
> Is there a new activity that you would like to be available in your area?
>
> We'll publish the best articles answering these questions next month.

Write your **article**.

Question 3

Your English teacher has asked you to write a story.
Your story must begin with this sentence.

As I came out of the supermarket, I saw someone that I had wanted to see for a long time.

Write your **story**.

LISTENING (approximately 30 minutes)

Part 1

Questions 1–7

For each question, choose the correct answer.

---

1   What has the man forgotten to pack for the trip?

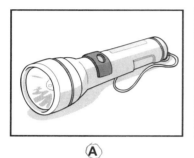
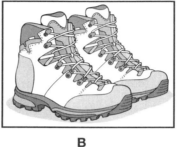
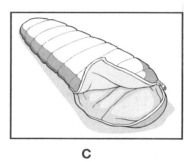

     A   B   C

2   What time is the plane expected to depart?

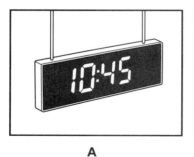

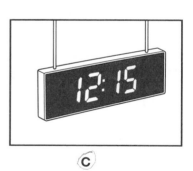

     A   B   C

3   Where did the family go at the weekend?

     A   B   C

4   What are the man and woman going to order?

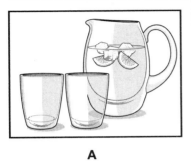

A

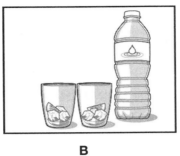

B

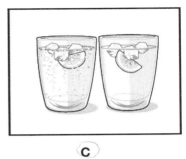

C

5   Which photograph did the man take?

A

B

C

6   How does the man suggest his friends should travel to the concert?

A

B

C

7   What is the weather forecast for the north this morning?

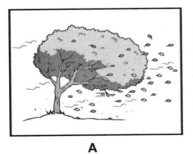

A

B

C

Part 2

Questions 8–13

For each question, choose the correct answer.

---

8   You will hear a boy telling a friend about plans for his birthday.
How does he feel about the plans he's made?

    A   annoyed that some of his friends don't want to come

    B   disappointed that he can't invite more friends

    C   worried that it might be boring for his friends

9   You will hear two friends talking about a football match they went to.
They both think that

    A   the crowd was smaller than usual.

    B   the match was quite boring.

    C   the referee made some bad decisions.

10   You will hear a man telling his friend about a skiing holiday.
How did he feel during the holiday?

    A   upset that he was injured

    B   embarrassed by his skiing ability

    C   angry that his friends put photos online

11   You will hear two friends talking about cars.
The woman thinks the best way to get information about new cars is from

    A   advertisements.

    B   TV programmes.

    C   internet reviews.

12 You will hear a woman telling a friend about a singing competition.
What does the woman say about it?

    A   Judging it is the easiest part.

    B   It is taking a long time to organise it.

    C   She would love to perform in it.

13 You will hear a woman talking to a friend about her recent move to a city.
How does the woman feel about it?

    A   pleased about a surprising health benefit

    B   glad that she has met friendly people

    C   satisfied with her local area

Part 3

Questions 14–19

For each question, write the correct answer in the gap.
Write **one** or **two words** or a **number** or a **date** or a **time**.

You will hear a woman called Kelly Robinson talking about her work as a maker of cartoon films.

The maker of cartoon films

Kelly did a degree in **(14)** ...art... at university.

Kelly really enjoys going to work because of the **(15)** ...Software... at the company.

Kelly's department is responsible for creating **(16)** ...animals... in cartoons.

At the moment Kelly is trying to develop her **(17)** ...new... skills.

It takes Kelly's company **(18)** ...two years... to make a full-length cartoon film.

Kelly's next project will be some cartoons for a **(19)** ...website... .

Part 4

Questions 20–25

For each question, choose the correct answer.

You will hear an interview with a girl called Rosie Banks, who swims in international competitions.

20 Rosie swam a lot when she was very young because

    A   her father thought it was an important skill.

    B   she wanted to be like her brother.

    C   there were free classes at her local pool.

21 What did Rosie dislike about doing serious swimming training?

    A   being away from her friends

    B   the long journey from home

    C   missing some school lessons

22 When Rosie won the Swim Stars International competition she was

    A   surprised by the public interest.

    B   amazed that she had done so well.

    C   excited about meeting other famous sportspeople.

23 Rosie says she needs more help with the cost of

    A   transport to competitions.

    B   the kit she needs.

    C   her accommodation while she's abroad.

24 What has Rosie changed since she got a new coach?

    A   her swimming style

    B   what she eats

    C   her fitness routine

25 What is Rosie planning to do in Spain?

    A   take part in some races

    B   train with different people

    C   have some time to relax

Test 3

READING (45 minutes)

Part 1

Questions 1–5

For each question, choose the correct answer.

1

Zara should

A buy something for Ali's dinner.

B have dinner without Ali.

C eat the dinner that Ali has made.

2

What does the seller say?

A The items he has got are not all in perfect condition.

B You can contact him any time you like.

C His furniture is not made in an old-fashioned style.

3

This tennis equipment is for club members only.
To hire rackets and balls for use on the court, see Reception.

A You're not permitted to use this equipment unless you have club membership.

B If you wish to become a member of the tennis club, ask at Reception.

C Non-members must bring their own equipment to use on these courts.

4

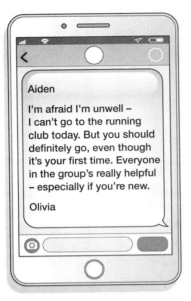

Aiden

I'm afraid I'm unwell – I can't go to the running club today. But you should definitely go, even though it's your first time. Everyone in the group's really helpful – especially if you're new.

Olivia

A Olivia is encouraging Aiden to go running today.

B Olivia wants Aiden to tell the group that she can't run today.

C Olivia is letting Aiden know that the running group are expecting him today.

5

College Art Class

To prepare for next lesson, find out about famous landscape paintings so you can discuss them in class. We'll also use computers to look at pictures painted outdoors to inspire us.

A Students will be working outdoors during their next art class.

B Students must produce their next picture using painting software.

C Students should do some research before the next session.

Part 2

Questions 6–10

For each question, choose the correct answer.

The people below all want to find a castle to visit.
On the opposite page there are descriptions of eight castles.
Decide which castle would be the most suitable for the people below.

6

Alan is keen on history, and wants to visit a castle that was the site of well-known historical events. He'd like the castle to be near the coast, with tours led by a guide.

7

Yoshiko wants to see a castle that people are still living in. She loves visiting beautiful gardens, and would like to explore interesting places in the castle.

8

Paulo and Maria collect antiques, so want to visit a castle that still has some of its original furniture on display, and hear about the building's history. They also want something that's particularly suitable for young children.

9

Kerim wants somewhere with a great historical atmosphere, with typical food from the past to try, and people dressed in costume. He'd also like to see art that's been in the castle for centuries.

10

Jake and his brother have always wanted to visit the ruins of a castle surrounded by water, with great views. Jake also wants to learn about any wildlife living in and around the castle.

Castles to visit

A **Durston Castle** has a valuable art collection, secret tunnels – one leading to the beach – and visitors mustn't miss the unusual rooms deep beneath the castle walls. Because the building is the Durston family's home, some parts cannot be visited – but you can sit on the grass under the trees and admire the flower beds and fountains. There's a play area for children too.

B At **Castle Woodward,** experience what life was like at the time it was built. Staff wear clothes typical of the time, and offer everyone tasty snacks made using recipes from different periods of history. Inside, the walls are covered with original paintings of the generations of people who've lived in the castle.

C **Castle Hemsworth**'s guides, dressed in historical costumes, give visitors information about the traditional castle building, towers and gardens. Wild horses live nearby. Inside, the castle looks unchanged, with old furniture and portraits of people who've lived here.

D Only a few parts of the ancient castle of **Marlin** are left, but you can still visit some underground rooms and see beautiful countryside from the high tower. The castle is in the middle of a lake and has lovely gardens. There are talks about the castle, and the bats, birds and butterflies that have made Marlin their home.

E **Chartsmouth Castle** was once owned and lived in by kings. Visitors love exploring the rooms, some of which have hidden tunnels. You can see the sea from the top of the walls, and younger visitors will love the outdoor games.

F Experts at the ruins of **Carston Castle** will show you around and give you information – and offer you 17th-century snacks! Hear how the building was once the scene of famous battles, and is now home to a variety of wildlife. And from the south side, there are fantastic sea views.

G **Rushford** is an old castle on the coast which is a popular local attraction. The Rushford Castle café in the walls serves food typical of the castle's history. Inside, there are beautiful rooms with antique tables and clocks. Outside, visitors can see a wide variety of wildlife.

H Sawbridge Castle was built in 1712 on an island in a lake. Inside, you can still see beautifully designed beds, tables and other objects once used by families living there. Put on headphones and listen to information about the history of Sawbridge Castle. Visitors of all ages will love the toy museum in the gardens.

Part 3

Questions 11–15

For each question, choose the correct answer.

Ana Ronson

Singer-songwriter

Singer-songwriter Ana Ronson grew up in Ireland. Although her parents weren't musicians, there was always music in the house. Her grandfather played the guitar, and taught Ana and her brother to play.

The first time Ana tried singing in front of an audience was at school – she was so nervous that her teacher had to lead her off the stage. This teacher suggested that joining the school theatre club might make her more confident. After attending the club for a while, she happily sang with 50 other students at an end-of-term concert.

A year later, her brother, who was in a band, asked her to write a song for them, and so she wrote her first ever song, *Falling Stars*. Writing it took just three days and she enjoyed it so much that she enrolled on a songwriting course run by a professional songwriter. Despite being the youngest student, she already knew more about music than many of the others. But Ana says the teacher didn't listen to anything she said, and she wrote *Something to Say* about how annoyed this made her feel.

She posted this song online, and it became a huge success. She was delighted when people left comments saying that they loved it and found new meanings in the words each time they heard them. Joss Alton, the owner of a recording company called Isotope Music, flew from his office on the other side of Ireland to ask her to join Isotope. At first she wasn't sure; she didn't know anything about the company, and didn't want someone telling her what to sing. However, Joss persuaded her this wouldn't happen, and a short time later she performed at a concert in Dublin arranged by Isotope. They sold all the tickets very quickly and it was an amazing evening.

Ana says she's less interested in writing songs about when life's good; when it's not, there's more for her to say. One of her favourite songs is *Decision*, written about why her brother stopped singing for a while, and how unhappy it made him. While she hopes that fans will like her songs, her aim is to write about personal experiences that matter to her.

11   What helped Ana stop being scared of singing to an audience?

    A   practising her singing with a band

    B   asking a teacher to stand on stage with her

    C   being in a drama group at school

    D   making sure she was not in the front row

12   How was the songwriting course useful for Ana?

    A   She was able to meet some well-known singers.

    B   The teacher's attitude gave her an idea for a song.

    C   She learnt a lot from other writers on the course.

    D   The teacher gave her advice about the music business.

13   Ana decided to work with Joss Alton because

    A   he promised to let her choose which songs to sing.

    B   he offered to help her put on a concert.

    C   she liked some other singers that he worked with.

    D   he owned a company in her home town.

14   Ana most enjoys writing songs that

    A   she is sure her fans will like.

    B   deal with difficult times.

    C   her brother can sing with his band.

    D   help people remember their own experiences.

15   What would Ana write to fans in her blog?

A Listening to my parents playing music on their instruments really encouraged me to become a singer myself.	**B** Writing songs just gets easier with practice. Nowadays it only takes a week or so – it wasn't like that when I started!
C I loved playing the concert in Dublin. I hope that next time we'll sell all the tickets – it was a shame to have some empty seats!	**D** I read what people write about me online – it means a lot to me that they like listening carefully to my songs.

Part 4

Questions 16–20

Five sentences have been removed from the text below.
For each question, choose the correct answer.
There are three extra sentences which you do not need to use.

Steve Dalway's cycle ride

Steve Dalway has recently completed an amazing bike ride between the US cities of Los Angeles and Boston, a distance of nearly 5,500 km. He and ten other cyclists took part in a trip organised by a company that provided a mechanic, planned the accommodation and route, and carried the cyclists' bags. **16** [____] Even with these, the ride involved a huge amount of effort.

Steve had already completed another long cycle ride in Europe. **17** [____] For example, he knew that on any ride, eating properly is important. When you don't eat enough, your ability to recover after hard exercise is reduced. For this reason, he always made sure he had a large breakfast before setting off every morning. **18** [____] The sight of the hotel at the end of the day was still very welcome, however!

One of the toughest times for the riders in the US was when the route climbed high into the Rocky Mountains. By the end of that part of the ride, Steve had climbed an amazing 28,000 m in total.

19 [____] An early section of the ride, for instance, took the group of cyclists through the Mojave desert, where the high temperatures made them feel as if they were in an oven. In the desert, Steve had to drink four litres of liquid every 40 km in order to keep going.

The cyclists used paper maps and had electronic devices to record the distances they travelled. So that everyone knew what they'd be facing the next day, a big map was displayed every evening in the hotel where the group were staying. **20** [____] At first the cyclists were disappointed when the black line drawn on the map by the organisers only moved forward by small amounts, despite all the day's work. At the end of the ride, however, they felt very proud of what they'd achieved.

A   He therefore had an idea of what to expect on this one.

B   It also allowed them to see the progress they had made.

C   He was surprised that he had gone so fast.

D   Doing that gave him the energy he needed to keep going.

E   It also arranged stops every 50 km for snacks and drinks.

F   This ride would be 1,000 km longer.

G   As a result, Steve's family knew how he was feeling each day.

H   There were other challenges, too.

Part 5

Questions 21–26

For each question, choose the correct answer.

Honey

People all over the world enjoy eating honey. But how much do you know about this **(21)** .... food? Most honey is made by bees, but what few people realise is that there are several types of bee which make honey.

Bees may have to visit about two million flowers to produce only half a kilo of honey. The type of flower the bees visit **(22)** .... both how the honey tastes and its colour. In fact, there are **(23)** .... more than three hundred kinds of honey.

In **(24)** .... times, honey was added to food instead of sugar, as sugar was very rare. In many cultures, people have used it for centuries to **(25)** .... various health problems. **(26)** ...., people all over the world still add it to hot water and drink it when they have a sore throat.

21	A	usual	B	shared	C	general	D	common
22	A	makes	B	affects	C	guides	D	directs
23	A	correctly	B	actually	C	accurately	D	absolutely
24	A	antique	B	far	C	elderly	D	ancient
25	A	cure	B	mend	C	repair	D	assist
26	A	Recently	B	Lately	C	Nowadays	D	Already

Part 6

Questions 27–32

For each question, write the correct answer.
Write **one** word for each gap.

Starting at college

Hi, my name's Emma. Welcome to the college! I've been studying here for a year now.
Starting at college isn't easy, but I'm sure you'll soon feel at home. When I first started
studying here last year, I was **(27)** .... nervous that I couldn't even ask
anyone for help. I got lost five times on my first day!

Remember that **(28)** .... student at the college has been new at one time,
and understands how you feel. So **(29)** .... you're not sure where to go, just
ask – we're all happy to help!

You probably don't know many people here. To make some friends, **(30)** ....
not spend break times with some of your new classmates in the café? Or how
(31) .... joining one of the many clubs we have at the college?
(32) .... are lots to choose from.

Good luck on your new course!

WRITING (45 minutes)

Part 1

You **must** answer this question.
Write your answer in about **100 words** on the answer sheet.

Question 1

Read this email from your college English teacher Miss Jones and the notes you have made.

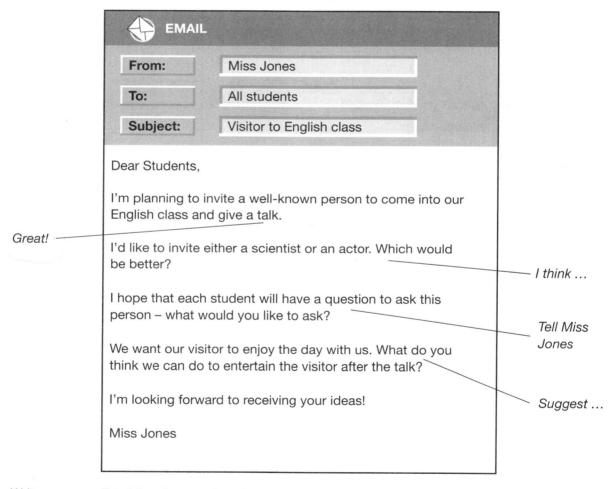

Write your **email** to Miss Jones using **all the notes**.

Part 2

Choose **one** of these questions.
Write your answer in about **100 words** on the answer sheet.

Question 2

You see this announcement in an English-language magazine.

Articles wanted!

Computer games

Do you and your friends enjoy playing computer games?
What are the good and bad things about computer games?

The most interesting articles answering these questions will appear in our magazine.

Write your **article**.

Question 3

Your English teacher has asked you to write a story.
Your story must begin with this sentence.

It was my first time in the jungle and I was so excited.

Write your **story**.

LISTENING (approximately 30 minutes)

Part 1

Questions 1–7

For each question, choose the correct answer.

1   Why was the man late?

A

B

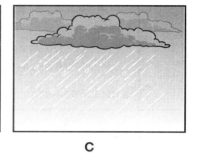

C

2   Why is the main road closed today?

A

B

C

3   Where do they decide to have the wedding anniversary party?

A

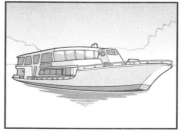

B

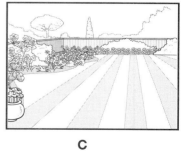

C

4   What does the man decide to order?

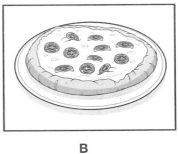

A   B   C

5   Which armchair is the man going to buy?

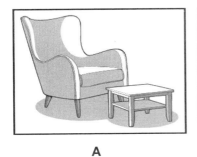
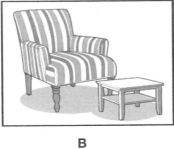
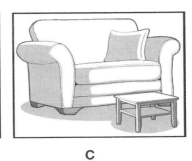

A   B   C

6   Which concert has the woman arranged to attend?

A   B   C

7   Which tomatoes will the man use?

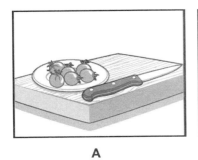
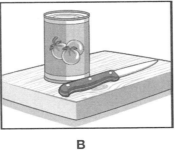
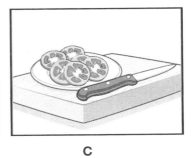

A   B   C

Part 2

Questions 8–13

For each question, choose the correct answer.

---

8 You will hear two friends talking about doing exercise.
Why is the man finding it difficult to do exercise?

   A   He can't afford to go to the gym.

   B   He doesn't have a lot of free time.

   C   There aren't any sports facilities nearby.

9 You will hear two people talking in a restaurant.
They agree that

   A   the soup was very spicy.

   B   the fish dishes were very tasty.

   C   one of the desserts was very small.

10 You will hear a woman telling her friend about her neighbours.
What problem does she have with her neighbours?

   A   They are noisy.

   B   They are unfriendly.

   C   They are untidy.

11 You will hear two friends talking about a new museum.
What does the woman say about it?

   A   She was surprised by some things on display.

   B   The opening hours suit her.

   C   She hopes to have another chance to visit.

12 You will hear a man talking to a colleague about a hotel he stayed in.
He complains that

A the room was too small for him.

B the location wasn't what he expected.

C he was disturbed by the traffic.

13 You will hear two passengers talking on an aeroplane.
How does the woman feel about flying?

A She thinks it's very convenient.

B She finds it a relaxing way to travel.

C She prefers travelling by train to flying.

Part 3

Questions 14–19

For each question, write the correct answer in the gap.
Write **one** or **two words** or a **number** or a **date** or a **time**.

You will hear a tour guide talking about arrangements for a day trip to a place called Gulum.

Day trip to Gulum

Bus leaves at: **(14)** .... a.m.

Meet before trip at: hotel **(15)** ....

First stop: ruin of a **(16)** ....

Lunch at: The **(17)** .... Restaurant

Afternoon activity: **(18)** .... or beach volleyball

Bring: **(19)** ....

Part 4

Questions 20–25

For each question, choose the correct answer.

You will hear an interview with a man called James Sweeney who works as a tree-climbing instructor.

20 How did James become interested in trees?

    A   He worked for someone who looked after trees.

    B   He enjoyed playing in trees when he was a child.

    C   He learnt about trees from his mother.

21 What surprised James when he first learnt to climb trees?

    A   the time it took to become good at it

    B   the wide range of people in the class

    C   the amount of equipment needed

22 What does James enjoy most about his teaching work?

    A   helping people who need the skill for their work

    B   giving people an interesting new experience

    C   showing people how to climb in different kinds of weather

23 James travels around the USA a lot because

    A   interest in tree climbing is increasing there.

    B   there isn't much work in his own area in winter.

    C   he'd like to visit as many parts of the country as possible.

24 What does James like about sleeping in trees?

    A   He wakes up to the sound of birds.

    B   He thinks it's comfortable.

    C   He can look at the stars.

25 When James climbs in the rainforests, he moves more slowly because

    A   he wants to study the insects.

    B   he finds the trees difficult to climb.

    C   he has to protect the trees.

Test 4

READING (45 minutes)

Part 1

Questions 1–5

For each question, choose the correct answer.

1

Why is Anne texting?

A to ask Eric if he can do her a favour

B to remind Eric about what they have agreed

C to give Eric an update regarding their arrangement

2

A Students of any year group are able to come to the careers talk.

B Students should go to the talk if they need help applying for a job.

C Students must register quickly because places at the event are limited.

3

Recycling Centre Users

Glass, plastic and metal items must be cleaned before you bring them to the recycling centre. Please place them in the correct recycling bin – the recycling centre staff are there to help.

A Recycling centre staff will clean items for recycling.

B Certain items need to be washed before they are recycled.

C All items can be placed in the same recycling bin.

4

Nora

You know the silent disco we spoke about? You've got to wear their special headphones so you can hear the DJ. Besides you, who else should I get tickets for? They're running out!

Gabriel

A Gabriel has got a ticket for Nora to go to the special dance event.

B Gabriel is informing Nora that she needs to remember to bring headphones.

C Gabriel wants Nora to suggest who may be interested in going to the disco.

5

If you need information about the ingredients in any of our dishes, please tell your waiter when you are choosing food from our menu.

A Our staff can let you know about what we've used to make our dishes.

B Read the information on our menu if you need to avoid eating certain ingredients.

C Tell your waiter if you'd prefer something different from what's on the menu.

Part 2

Questions 6–10

For each question, choose the correct answer.

The people below all want to see a musical show at the theatre.
On the opposite page there are eight reviews of shows.
Decide which show would be the most suitable for the people below.

6  Erika wants to see a show with music and which has famous actors in the lead roles. She'd like it to be based on a book and contain many different types of music.

7  Guillermo would like to go to a show that's funny and is about a real person. He's looking for one with some music in it, but with more speaking than singing.

8 Neelam wants to see a musical show which contains lots of special effects and would like to watch it in an unusual place. She'd like to see a love story.

9  Oumar wants to go to a show that's a bit frightening. He'd like to see a story set in the past and realistic costumes from the period.

10 Mira wants a show with dancing, as well as songs by well-known musicians. She'd like the music to be in a range of styles from around the world.

The best musical shows in town

A   Glad!

Glad! tells the story of a teenage girl whose dreams of becoming a famous musician come true with the help of some special (and amusing!) friends. The costumes and songs are amazing, and although it's fiction, it has the feel of a real-life story. It's on for one week only, on a temporary stage in the football stadium.

B   Mary Wright

The two well-known lead actors in this 16th-century drama are surprisingly good dancers, and the music creates quite a scary atmosphere. The clothes by top designer Jean-Luc Filbert are historically accurate and look absolutely wonderful.

C   The Amazing Mr Mason

This unusual musical is based on a famous story written over 400 years ago. The hero falls in love with a princess who's forced to move to another country. There's quite a lot of speaking for a musical, but the ending's a surprising pleasure.

D   The End of Summer

You've probably read the novel which this musical comedy takes its story from, but you won't recognise the songs, as they were specially written for the show. Several songwriters were needed, due to the wide variety of music the producers wanted. The stars, who you'll probably recognise from TV, are fantastic.

E   Keeping Time

Keeping Time is based on the real-life story of the popular group *Marcellous*, and includes their best work. We see how having members from three different continents allowed them to create songs using music from each place. Unusually, there's ballet in this show, but it goes surprisingly well with their music.

F   No Exit

With its use of film and advanced technology to make it seem like the characters appear in two places at once, this spectacular musical starts off as an old-fashioned ghost story but quickly turns into a highly entertaining romantic comedy. The fact that the show is performed in an old factory building only adds to the enjoyment.

G   Tiger Prince

The Tiger Prince leaves his jungle home and comes to the city in this fabulous musical. The story isn't particularly original but the computer-controlled light show goes perfectly with the amazing dance routines to make this a must-see show.

H   The Final Whistle

If you're tired of serious dramas and dull love stories, why not give this laugh-a-minute show a try? The true story of basketball player Andy Hammond is cleverly told. Despite being advertised as a musical show, it actually has very few songs. You'll love all the brilliant jokes and entertaining conversations.

Part 3

Questions 11–15

For each question, choose the correct answer.

My Canadian trip

by Louise Walton

Last year I went on an amazing trip – travelling by boat on a guided group tour along the west coast of Canada. It was my brother Harry's idea. He's a journalist, like me, and he wanted to write articles about the trip. He's also a great fan of boats, although that's one interest we definitely don't share. But I'd dreamt of visiting the area ever since seeing it on TV as a child, especially as I knew it was where our great-grandparents had lived before moving to Europe. So I kept asking Harry if I could go too – until he finally agreed!

A few weeks before we left home, there were storms in the area we were going to. But luckily the forecast for the time we intended to be there was for calm seas. Although there was plenty to arrange, I was busy at work so didn't have much time to think about what needed doing. But Harry promised he'd taken care of everything, so I knew everything would be all right.

After arriving in Canada, we joined the group, packed our limited supplies into small boats and set off. The guide had mentioned that very few people now lived along that coast, and sure enough, the only other living creatures we saw for the first few days were dolphins and birds. We knew there were islands in the distance, but the early-morning fog made it hard to see very far, so I just focussed on the beautiful patterns our boat made in the water.

We often stopped for hours to explore the rock pools on the beaches. They were full of amazing coloured fish, many of which I didn't recognise. And it was great to be able to stop caring about how quickly or slowly the day was passing. We never forgot lunch or dinner, though, which we all made together over camp fires. When we finally fell asleep on the boats each evening, even though the beds were hard, it really felt like stress-free living!

When the time came to leave, I was sad. How could I return to normal life again? But I knew if I stayed, I'd miss family and friends. I was also looking forward to telling everyone at home about our adventures!

---

11 Why was Louise keen to go on the trip to Canada?

    A   She liked the idea of spending time in a boat.

    B   She knew her brother wanted her to accompany him.

    C   She had wanted to travel there for a long time.

    D   She had heard from some relatives who lived there.

12 Just before their departure, Louise

    A   began to wonder how they would deal with bad weather.

    B   was confident that they were fully prepared for the trip.

    C   wished she could help her brother more.

    D   felt she was better organised than usual.

13 On the first morning of the trip, Louise says she admired

    A   the way the sea around them looked.

    B   the wildlife which their boats attracted.

    C   the homes that people had built in the area.

    D   the views of islands they were passing.

14 During the trip, Louise enjoyed

    A   learning the names of the fish she saw.

    B   not having to cook regular meals.

    C   spending the nights in comfort.

    D   not having to worry about time.

15 What would Louise write in her diary during the trip?

A
> There are wonderful pools along the coast, left behind by the sea. I wish we had the time to look at them more carefully.

B
> I can't believe I'm in the same place I saw on that programme ages ago. Our great-grandparents would be amazed!

C
> We've brought a lot of stuff with us in the boats – I'm sure it's not all necessary. It's surprising they don't sink!

D
> It'll be hard to say goodbye to the place at the end, but I can't wait to get back to work – I've really missed it.

Part 4

Questions 16–20

For each question, choose the correct answer.

The Museum of Trash

In an industrial area in California, in the USA, large garbage trucks regularly deliver tons of rubbish to a recycling centre. Meanwhile, coaches deliver crowds of people who are coming to visit *The Museum of Trash*. **16** [   ] It is a colourful elephant made entirely out of rubbish.

The unusual sculpture was created out of all sorts of rubbish: old signs, mobile phones, shoes, sunglasses, plastic toys, car number plates, and anything else that the artist could get his hands on.

17 [   ] They have fun trying to find them all. The sculpture is 4 metres tall and weighs around 900 kg, which is equal to the average amount of rubbish each person in California throws away every year. **18** [   ]

While the elephant sculpture is popular, visitors also enjoy being able to see what happens at a real recycling centre. Rubbish which can be recycled is brought here every day. **19** [   ] People who live in these places are happy to know that what they throw away will not be wasted. Once it has arrived at the recycling centre, the rubbish is put into separate containers according to what it is made from, and sold to businesses that can use it to create new products. The companies make a range of things out of the recycled materials, and some of them can be bought in the museum shop.

'What is really exciting is that people go home and tell their friends what they can recycle,' says the museum's director. '**20** [   ] They can see where all the rubbish goes and learn that recycling is better than just wasting things.'

A	Few of these items were recycled into anything that people could wear.
B	Visitors are given a list of the different objects in it.
C	Although this might not seem like a lot, it is more than in most museums.
D	So while it is fun for visitors, they also pass on their new knowledge.
E	It comes from twenty towns in the local area.
F	Nowadays, however, over 30,000 visitors come to the museum each year.
G	The first display they see looks like something out of an animated movie.
H	It is certainly shocking to see what that actually looks like.

Part 5

Questions 21–26

For each question, choose the correct answer.

Inventing the telephone

The telephone was invented by Alexander Graham Bell. His first career involved teaching people how to use a system which his father had **(21)** .... to help deaf people communicate. Because of this, Bell became more and more interested in all types of communication.

Bell wanted to **(22)** .... it possible for people to talk to each other over **(23)** .... distances. He realised that he had to turn sound into electricity and then back to sound again. This was a big engineering **(24)** ....

In 1876, after several months of hard work on this problem, Bell and his assistant Thomas Watson **(25)** .... it.

The first words ever spoken on the telephone are famous. Bell was working on their new invention in his laboratory when he accidentally **(26)** .... dangerous liquid on his clothes. He called Watson and said, 'Come here, I want to see you!'

21	**A** thought	**B** developed	**C** done	**D** reached
22	**A** create	**B** have	**C** get	**D** make
23	**A** long	**B** high	**C** wide	**D** far
24	**A** request	**B** demand	**C** challenge	**D** method
25	**A** solved	**B** answered	**C** succeeded	**D** found
26	**A** lost	**B** kept	**C** fell	**D** spilt

Part 6

Questions 27–32

For each question, write the correct answer.
Write **one** word for each gap.

From: Harry

To: Oliver

Subject: Piano lessons

Hi Oliver,

Guess what? I've finally started piano lessons, like you! As you know, it's something I've wanted to do ever **(27)** .... I was young. Anyway, a couple of months ago I saw someone playing the piano on TV – he was brilliant. And when I found out he'd only started playing quite recently, that encouraged **(28)** .... to start lessons.

I've got a really good teacher, and I go to her house twice a week **(29)** .... lessons. She's very patient. Every time I make a mistake, she explains what I did wrong. Also, I couldn't read music when I started. It's been hard to learn to read the notes on the page and decide which piano keys to use at the **(30)** .... time! But when I finally play something that other people recognise, it really makes me happy. Maybe **(31)** .... day, I'll become even better **(32)** .... you are at playing the piano!

WRITING (45 minutes)

Part 1

You **must** answer this question.
Write your answer in about **100 words** on the answer sheet.

Question 1

Read this email from your English-speaking friend Jo and the notes you have made.

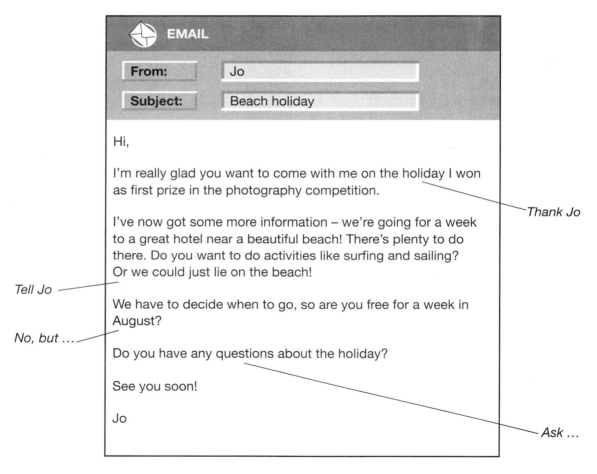

Write your **email** to Jo using **all the notes**.

Part 2

Choose **one** of these questions.
Write your answer in about **100 words** on the answer sheet.

Question 2

You see this announcement in an English-language magazine.

Articles wanted!

Learning languages

Do you think it's important to learn a foreign language?
Is it better to learn a language in a group or on your own? Why?

We'll publish the most interesting articles answering these questions in our magazine.

Write your **article**.

Question 3

Your English teacher has asked you to write a story.
Your story must begin with this sentence.

The friends got off the bus and ran over to join the long queue of people.

Write your **story**.

LISTENING   (approximately 30 minutes)

Part 1

Questions 1–7

For each question, choose the correct answer.

---

1   How will the man travel to the city centre?

  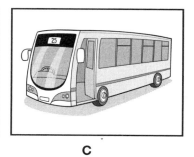

A   **B**   **C**

2   What did the girl dislike at the hostel she stayed in?

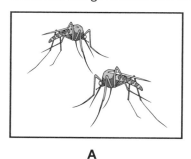 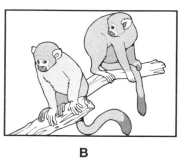 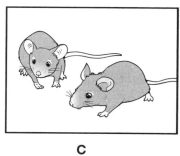

A   **B**   **C**

3   What is the man going to order for lunch?

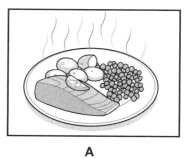  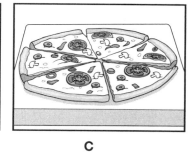

A   **B**   **C**

4 What sport would the woman like to try?

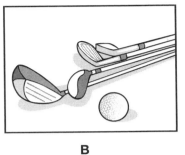

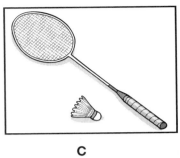

A   B   C

5 Which book is the man reading?

A   B   C

6 Where does the man suggest going at the weekend?

A   B   C

7 How much is the latest smartphone in the store today?

A   B   C

Part 2

Questions 8–13

For each question, choose the correct answer.

8   You will hear a brother and sister talking about a gift for their cousin.
    Why do they decide to buy the gift online?

    A   It's heavy to carry home from the shop.

    B   It's not available in the shop.

    C   It's difficult to get to the shop.

9   You will hear two colleagues discussing their holiday travel plans.
    The man thinks that the woman should

    A   go somewhere new for her holiday.

    B   spend more time away.

    C   take a different type of transport.

10   You will hear a man talking to a friend about a fitness training session.
    The man cannot attend today's session because

    A   his doctor has advised him to rest.

    B   he has not recovered from a cold yet.

    C   he has just had an operation.

11   You will hear two friends talking about a play they've just seen.
    What does the woman say about the play?

    A   It improved after the interval.

    B   The costumes were strange.

    C   The acting was disappointing.

12   You will hear two friends talking about a film and its soundtrack.
      What does the woman say about the soundtrack?

    A   It's enjoyable for all ages.

    B   It's relaxing to listen to.

    C   It's better than the film.

13   You will hear two friends talking about the news.
      They agree that

    A   reading the news is an essential part of the day.

    B   it's best to read the news online.

    C   there's too much news about famous people.

Part 3

Questions 14–19

For each question, write the correct answer in the gap.
Write **one** or **two words** or a **number** or a **date** or a **time**.

You will hear a guide giving some information about a walk in the countryside.

Countryside walk

The walk will take **(14)** .... hours.

Walkers should be careful of **(15)** .... along the route.

Walkers will have lunch near the **(16)** ....

Walkers are likely to see wildlife including **(17)** ....

At the end of the walk, people can visit a **(18)** ....

It's possible to take a **(19)** .... back to the place where the walk started.

Part 4

Questions 20–25

For each question, choose the correct answer.

You will hear an interview with a young poet called Laura Dickson.

20 Laura first became interested in poetry

    A   by reading it at home.

    B   by studying it at school.

    C   by learning about it from her father.

21 What made Laura decide to become a professional poet?

    A   She met a famous poet.

    B   She did a poetry course.

    C   She won a poetry prize.

22 What is Laura's new book about?

    A   various types of buildings

    B   personal relationships

    C   climate change

23 What does Laura say about reading poetry written a long time ago?

    A   She admires how well it's written.

    B   She finds it difficult to understand.

    C   She prefers to read modern poems.

24 How does Laura feel about her new job teaching at a university?

    A   pleased with her ability to do it well

    B   grateful to have helpful colleagues

    C   surprised by the amount of work

25 In the future, Laura would like to

    A   organise a poetry festival.

    B   take a break from writing poetry.

    C   add music to some of her poetry.

Speaking tests

Test 1

Note: The visual materials for Speaking Test 1 appear on pages 152 and 153.

Part 1 (2–3 minutes)

Phase 1
Interlocutor

To both candidates	Good morning/afternoon/evening. Can I have your mark sheets, please? *Hand over the mark sheets to the Assessor* I'm .... and this is ....
To Candidate A	What's your name? Where do you live/come from? Thank you.
To Candidate B	And what's your name? Where do you live/come from? Thank you.

	Back-up prompts
B, do you work or are you a student?	Do you have a job? Do you study?
What do you do/study?	What job do you do? What subject do you study?
Thank you.	
And **A**, do you work or are you a student?	Do you have a job? Do you study?
What do you do/study?	What job do you do? What subject do you study?
Thank you.	

Phase 2

Interlocutor

Select one or more questions from the list to ask each candidate.
Ask Candidate A first.

Back-up prompts

Which day of the week do you like the most? (Why?)

Which day do you like the most? (Why?)

What did you do yesterday evening/last weekend?

Did you do anything yesterday evening/last weekend? What?

Do you think that English will be useful for you in the future? (Why/Why not?)

Will you use English in the future? (Why?/Why not?)

Tell us about the people you live with.

Do you live with friends/your family?

What kind of websites do you like? (Why?)

What websites do you like? (Why?)

Which do you prefer, the morning or the afternoon? (Why?)

Which is better, morning or afternoon?

What kind of films do you like?

What films do you like?

What's your favourite type of music? (Why?)

Do you like rock music? (Why?/Why not?)

Thank you.

Part 2 (2–3 minutes)

A Having breakfast

Interlocutor	Now I'd like each of you to talk on your own about something. I'm going to give each of you a photograph and I'd like you to talk about it.
	A, here is your photograph. It shows **people having breakfast**.
	*Place **Part 2** booklet, open at **Task 1A**, in front of candidate.*
	B, you just listen. **A**, please tell us what you can see in the photograph.
Candidate A 🕐 *approx. 1 minute*	....
	Back-up prompts • Talk about the people/person. • Talk about the place. • Talk about other things in the photograph.
Interlocutor	Thank you. (Can I have the booklet, please?) *Retrieve **Part 2** booklet.*

B Cycling

Interlocutor	**B**, here is your photograph. It shows **people on bicycles**.
	*Place **Part 2** booklet, open at **Task 1B**, in front of candidate.*
	A, you just listen. **B**, please tell us what you can see in the photograph.
Candidate B 🕐 *approx. 1 minute*	....
	Back-up prompts • Talk about the people/person. • Talk about the place. • Talk about other things in the photograph.
Interlocutor	Thank you. (Can I have the booklet, please?) *Retrieve **Part 2** booklet.*

Reading and books

Parts 3 and 4 (6 minutes)

Part 3	
Interlocutor	Now, in this part of the test you're going to talk about something together for about two minutes. I'm going to describe a situation to you.
	*Place **Part 3** booklet, open at **Task 1C**, in front of the candidates.*
	A young man enjoys reading books about people with interesting lives. He is looking for a new book to read.
	Here are some books he could read.
	Talk together about the different books he could read and say which would be most interesting.
	All right? Now, talk together.
Candidates ⏱*approx. 2–3 minutes*	....
Interlocutor	Thank you. (Can I have the booklet, please?) *Retrieve **Part 3** booklet.*

Part 4	
Interlocutor	*Use the following questions, as appropriate:*

- **Do you like reading books about people with interesting lives? (Why?/Why not?)**

- **When was the last time you went to a bookshop? (Why?/Why not?)**

- **Have you ever bought a book as a present for someone? (Why?/Why not?)**

- **Do you prefer reading on a screen or reading printed books? (Why?/Why not?)**

- **Do you think people will still read printed books in the future? (Why?/Why not?)**

Select any of the following prompts, as appropriate:

- **How/what about you?**
- **Do you agree?**
- **What do you think?**

Thank you. That is the end of the test.

Test 2

Note: The visual materials for Speaking Test 2 appear on pages 154 and 155.

Part 1 (2–3 minutes)

Phase 1 **Interlocutor**	
To both candidates	Good morning/afternoon/evening. Can I have your mark sheets, please? *Hand over the mark sheets to the Assessor.* I'm ………… and this is ………… .
To Candidate A	What's your name? Where do you live/come from? Thank you.
To Candidate B	And what's your name? Where do you live/come from? Thank you.

	Back-up prompts
B, do you work or are you a student?	Do you have a job? Do you study?
What do you do/study?	What job do you do? What subject do you study?
Thank you.	
And **A**, do you work or are you a student?	Do you have a job? Do you study?
What do you do/study?	What job do you do? What subject do you study?
Thank you.	

Phase 2

Interlocutor

Select one or more questions from the list to ask each candidate.
Ask Candidate A first.

Back-up prompts

Which day of the week do you like
the most? (Why?)

Which day do you like the most? (Why?)

What did you do yesterday evening/last
weekend?

Did you do anything yesterday evening/last
weekend? What?

Do you think that English will be useful for
you in the future? (Why/Why not?)

Will you use English in the future?
(Why?/Why not?)

Tell us about the people you live with.

Do you live with friends/your family?

What kind of websites do you like? (Why?)

What websites do you like? (Why?)

Which do you prefer, the morning or the
afternoon? (Why?)

Which is better, morning or afternoon?

What kind of films do you like?

What films do you like?

What's your favourite type of music? (Why?)

Do you like rock music? (Why?/Why not?)

Thank you.

Part 2 (2–3 minutes)

A In the street

Interlocutor	Now I'd like each of you to talk on your own about something. I'm going to give each of you a photograph and I'd like you to talk about it. **A**, here is your photograph. It shows **people in the street**. *Place **Part 2** booklet, open at **Task 2A**, in front of candidate.* **B**, you just listen. **A**, please tell us what you can see in the photograph.
Candidate A 🕐 *approx. 1 minute*	………………………………………………………..

> **Back-up prompts**
> - Talk about the people/person.
> - Talk about the place.
> - Talk about other things in the photograph.

Interlocutor	Thank you. (Can I have the booklet, please?) *Retrieve **Part 2** booklet.*

B Museum visit

Interlocutor	**B**, here is your photograph. It shows **people visiting a museum**. *Place **Part 2** booklet, open at **Task 2B**, in front of candidate.* **A**, you just listen. **B**, please tell us what you can see in the photograph.
Candidate B 🕐 *approx. 1 minute*	…………………………………………………….

> **Back-up prompts**
> - Talk about the people/person.
> - Talk about the place.
> - Talk about other things in the photograph.

Interlocutor	Thank you. (Can I have the booklet, please?) *Retrieve **Part 2** booklet.*

Weather and travelling

Parts 3 and 4 (6 minutes)

Part 3

Interlocutor	Now, in this part of the test you're going to talk about something together for about two minutes. I'm going to describe a situation to you.
	*Place **Part 3** booklet, open at **Task 2C**, in front of the candidates.*
	A young woman is going to spend six months living and working in a cold country. Her friends would like to give her a present to take with her.
	Here are some presents they could give her.
	Talk together about the different presents her friends could give her and say which would be best.
	All right? Now, talk together.
Candidates ⏱ *approx. 2–3 minutes*	....
Interlocutor	Thank you. (Can I have the booklet, please?) *Retrieve **Part 3** booklet.*

Part 4

Interlocutor	*Use the following questions, as appropriate:*

- **Do you like cold weather? (Why?/Why not?)**

- **When you go on holiday, do you prefer to stay in your country or go to other countries? (Why?/Why not?)**

- **Is there a country you would really like to live in? (Why?/Why not?)**

- **How do you keep in contact with friends and family when you're away from home?**

- **Is it better to live in lots of different places or always live in the same place? (Why?)**

> *Select any of the following prompts, as appropriate:*
>
> - **How/what about you?**
> - **Do you agree?**
> - **What do you think?**

Thank you. That is the end of the test.

Test 3

Note: The visual materials for Speaking Test 3 appear on pages 156 and 157.

Part 1 (2–3 minutes)

Phase 1 **Interlocutor**	
To both candidates	Good morning/afternoon/evening. Can I have your mark sheets, please? *Hand over the mark sheets to the Assessor.* I'm .... and this is ....
To Candidate A	What's your name? Where do you live/come from? Thank you.
To Candidate B	And what's your name? Where do you live/come from? Thank you.

	Back-up prompts
B, do you work or are you a student?	Do you have a job? Do you study?
What do you do/study?	What job do you do? What subject do you study?
Thank you.	
And **A**, do you work or are you a student?	Do you have a job? Do you study?
What do you do/study?	What job do you do? What subject do you study?
Thank you.	

Phase 2

Interlocutor

Select one or more questions from the list to ask each candidate.
Ask Candidate A first.

Back-up prompts

Which day of the week do you like the most? (Why?)

Which day do you like the most? (Why?)

What did you do yesterday evening/last weekend?

Did you do anything yesterday evening/last weekend? What?

Do you think that English will be useful for you in the future? (Why/Why not?)

Will you use English in the future? (Why?/Why not?)

Tell us about the people you live with.

Do you live with friends/your family?

What kind of websites do you like? (Why?)

What websites do you like? (Why?)

Which do you prefer, the morning or the afternoon? (Why?)

Which is better, morning or afternoon?

What kind of films do you like?

What films do you like?

What's your favourite type of music? (Why?)

Do you like rock music? (Why?/Why not?)

Thank you.

Part 2 (2–3 minutes)

A Relaxing at home

Interlocutor	Now I'd like each of you to talk on your own about something. I'm going to give each of you a photograph and I'd like you to talk about it. **A**, here is your photograph. It shows **someone relaxing at home**. *Place **Part 2** booklet, open at **Task 3A**, in front of candidate.* **B**, you just listen. **A**, please tell us what you can see in the photograph.
Candidate A 🕐 *approx. 1 minute*	…………………………………………………..

> **Back-up prompts**
> • Talk about the people/person.
> • Talk about the place.
> • Talk about other things in the photograph.

Interlocutor	Thank you. (Can I have the booklet, please?) *Retrieve **Part 2** booklet.*

B Playing ice hockey

Interlocutor	**B**, here is your photograph. It shows **people playing ice hockey**. *Place **Part 2** booklet, open at **Task 3B**, in front of candidate.* **A**, you just listen. **B**, please tell us what you can see in the photograph.
Candidate B 🕐 *approx. 1 minute*	…………………………………………………….

> **Back-up prompts**
> • Talk about the people/person.
> • Talk about the place.
> • Talk about other things in the photograph.

Interlocutor	Thank you. (Can I have the booklet, please?) *Retrieve **Part 2** booklet.*

Buildings in a town

Parts 3 and 4 (6 minutes)

Part 3	
Interlocutor	Now, in this part of the test you're going to talk about something together for about two minutes. I'm going to describe a situation to you.
	*Place **Part 3** booklet, open at **Task 3C**, in front of the candidates.*
	A town has a large public building that is empty. The people in the town want to use the building.
	Here are some ideas for how to use the building.
	Talk together about the different ways the people of the town could use the empty building and say which would be best.
	All right? Now, talk together.
Candidates ⏱*approx. 2–3 minutes*	....
Interlocutor	Thank you. (Can I have the booklet, please?) *Retrieve **Part 3** booklet.*

Part 4	
Interlocutor	*Use the following questions, as appropriate:*

- **Where do you like going in your town? (Why?)**

- **Do you enjoy shopping in big department stores? (Why?/Why not?)**

- **When was the last time you went to the cinema?**

- **Do you prefer modern buildings or old buildings? (Why?)**

- **Is it important to look after old buildings? (Why?/Why not?)**

> *Select any of the following prompts, as appropriate:*
>
> - **How/what about you?**
> - **Do you agree?**
> - **What do you think?**

Thank you. That is the end of the test.

Test 4

Note: The visual materials for Speaking Test 4 appear on pages 158 and 159.

Part 1 (2–3 minutes)

Phase 1 **Interlocutor**	
To both candidates	Good morning/afternoon/evening. Can I have your mark sheets, please? *Hand over the mark sheets to the Assessor.* I'm .... and this is ....
To Candidate A	What's your name? Where do you live/come from? Thank you.
To Candidate B	And what's your name? Where do you live/come from? Thank you.

	Back-up prompts
B, do you work or are you a student?	Do you have a job? Do you study?
What do you do/study?	What job do you do? What subject do you study?
Thank you.	
And **A**, do you work or are you a student?	Do you have a job? Do you study?
What do you do/study?	What job do you do? What subject do you study?
Thank you.	

Phase 2
Interlocutor

Select one or more questions from the list to ask each candidate.
Ask Candidate A first.

	Back-up prompts
Which day of the week do you like the most? (Why?)	Which day do you like the most? (Why?)
What did you do yesterday evening/last weekend?	Did you do anything yesterday evening/last weekend? What?
Do you think that English will be useful for you in the future? (Why/Why not?)	Will you use English in the future? (Why?/Why not?)
Tell us about the people you live with.	Do you live with friends/your family?
What kind of websites do you like? (Why?)	What websites do you like? (Why?)
Which do you prefer, the morning or the afternoon? (Why?)	Which is better, morning or afternoon?
What kind of films do you like?	What films do you like?
What's your favourite type of music? (Why?)	Do you like rock music? (Why?/Why not?)

Thank you.

Part 2 (2–3 minutes)

A Saying goodbye

Interlocutor	Now I'd like each of you to talk on your own about something. I'm going to give each of you a photograph and I'd like you to talk about it.
	A, here is your photograph. It shows **people saying goodbye**.
	*Place **Part 2** booklet, open at **Task 4A**, in front of candidate.*
	B, you just listen. **A**, please tell us what you can see in the photograph.
Candidate A 🕐 *approx. 1 minute*	....

> **Back-up prompts**
> - Talk about the people/person.
> - Talk about the place.
> - Talk about other things in the photograph.

Interlocutor	Thank you. (Can I have the booklet, please?) *Retrieve **Part 2** booklet.*

B Shopping for shoes

Interlocutor	**B**, here is your photograph. It shows **people in a shop**.
	*Place **Part 2** booklet, open at **Task 4B**, in front of candidate.*
	A, you just listen. **B**, please tell us what you can see in the photograph.
Candidate B 🕐 *approx. 1 minute*	....

> **Back-up prompts**
> - Talk about the people/person.
> - Talk about the place.
> - Talk about other things in the photograph.

Interlocutor	Thank you. (Can I have the booklet, please?) *Retrieve **Part 2** booklet.*

The environment

Parts 3 and 4 (6 minutes)

Part 3

Interlocutor	Now, in this part of the test you're going to talk about something together for about two minutes. I'm going to describe a situation to you.
	Place **Part 3** *booklet, open at* **Task 4C**, *in front of the candidates.*
	A young man would like to do something to help the environment.
	Here are some things he could do.
	Talk together about the different things he could do to help the environment and say which would be best.
	All right? Now, talk together.
Candidates ⏱ *approx. 2–3 minutes*	....
Interlocutor	Thank you. (Can I have the booklet, please?) *Retrieve* **Part 3** *booklet.*

Part 4

Interlocutor	*Use the following questions, as appropriate:*

- **Did you learn about protecting the environment at school? (Why?/Why not?)**

- **Do you ever ride a bicycle? (Why?/Why not?)**

- **Do you like being in places with lots of trees? (Why?/Why not?)**

- **Would you like to recycle more things? (Why?/Why not?)**

- **Do you think people do enough to protect the environment? (Why?/Why not?)**

> *Select any of the following prompts, as appropriate:*
> - **How/what about you?**
> - **Do you agree?**
> - **What do you think?**

Thank you. That is the end of the test.

Test 1 answer key

Reading

Further feedback available in the downloadable resources

Part 1

1 B   **2** C   **3** A   **4** C   **5** B

Part 2

6 G   **7** C   **8** E   **9** B   **10** H

Part 3

11 C   **12** B   **13** D   **14** A   **15** C

Part 4

16 G   **17** D   **18** A   **19** B   **20** E

Part 5

21 A   **22** C   **23** D   **24** A   **25** B   **26** B

Part 6

27 It   **28** most   **29** all   **30** forward   **31** at   **32** if

Writing

Question 1

Sample answer A

Hi, Alex

I'm very glad to work with you. I think we shouldn't choose the rainforest as our topic because I'm not good at this topic. I would like to prepare the science presentation about deserts. In my opinion, it will be interesting.

Sorry, but my parents have gone to another town and I must look after my little brother so we can't start to prepare tomorrow. What about starting in 2 days?

We can prepare the presentation in my house because no one will disturb us.

I would prefer to give our presentation to the class in the afternoon as this is the most convenient time.

Gretta

Subscale	Mark	Commentary
Content	5	All content is relevant to the task. The target reader is fully informed about all four points in the task.
Communicative Achievement	5	The email is written in a consistently polite and friendly tone, *Hi, Alex*; *I'm very glad*; *I would like to*. Each point is addressed in an appropriate way and is often expanded. For example, in the second point, an apology is made and an explanation is given, followed by an alternative suggestion, *Sorry, but...so we can't...*; *What about...* The reader's attention would be held throughout and they would be able to make decisions based on the information in the email.
Organisation	5	The email is well-organised and coherent. There is good use of paragraphs and the information is clearly divided into separate sections. There is a variety of linking words and cohesive devices used to good effect, *our topic*; *because*; *this topic*; *In my opinion*; *Sorry, but*; *and*; *so*; *What about*; *in the afternoon as this is the most convenient time*. The references to information in the input material make the purpose for writing very clear.
Language	5	There is a range of vocabulary used which is suitable for the task, *deserts*; *interesting*; *look after*; *disturb*; *convenient*. The grammatical structures are used with control and a good degree of accuracy, *I think we shouldn't choose*; *it will be interesting*; *my parents have gone to*; *I must look after*; *we can't start to prepare*; *What about starting*; *no one will disturb us*; *as this is the most convenient time*.

Sample answer B

Hi!

I don't think it is a good idea that we doing the presentation about the rainforest, we need to do it about a subject which is not so common, so we don't have the same subject as someone else.

Sorry, but tomorrow I can't, I'm going to my grandpa & grandma to help with gardening.

I suggest that we prepare it at my place, so we can work quietly and concentrated.

I prefer it in the morning, so we are not nervous about it in the afternoon.

Anna

Subscale	Mark	Commentary
Content	5	All content is relevant to the task. The target reader is fully informed about the four points in the task.
Communicative Achievement	4	The register is appropriate for an email to a friend and straightforward ideas are communicated. Each point in the task has been responded to and reasons or explanations have been given to support the writer's opinion.
Organisation	3	The text is connected and coherent. Each sentence focuses on one of the points in the task and there is some evidence of linking words within sentences, *so*; *but*, and simple cohesive devices, *it*; *which*. Although paragraphing is clear, each one consists of only one sentence and there is little use of linking words at the beginning of each one to link them through the text. There are some errors with punctuation, particularly where commas are used to separate sentences rather than full stops, *about the rainforest, we need to*; *I can't, I'm going to*.
Language	3	Everyday vocabulary is used generally appropriately, *common*; *gardening*; *quietly*; *nervous*. Simple grammatical forms, such as the present simple and continuous and simple modal verbs, are used with a good degree of control, *we need to do it*; *so we don't have*; *I'm going to*; *so we can work*; *so we are not nervous about it*. There are some errors, *that we doing*; *concentrated*, but these do not impede communication.

Question 2

Sample answer A

Is shopping boring?

Most people like shopping, but other consider it to be a terrible waste of time. I like shopping for the ability of purchasing different useful things. I also like comparing sales in different shops. It helps me to decide where can I save more money. However, the process of shopping seems me to be too boring. Even fashionable shops don't entertain me at all if they have big queues there.

In my opinion, shopping centres should open more shops. Then queues will not be so enormous.

In conclusion, shopping is quite an amusing hobby, though it has some disadvantages. Shopping centres would be more entertaining if they will be improved.

Subscale	Mark	Commentary
Content	5	All content is relevant to the task. The target reader is fully informed as all questions in the task have been covered.
Communicative Achievement	5	The text is written in a suitable register for an article and the target reader's attention is held. Straightforward ideas, such as expressing personal opinions *I like shopping*; *I also like comparing*; *seems me to be too boring*, and making suggestions about how the experience of shopping could be improved are communicated clearly, *shopping centres should open more shops*.
Organisation	4	The text is generally well-organised, despite some minor errors with punctuation, *open more shops. Then*; *an amusing hobby, though*, and good use is made of paragraphs to focus on specific aspects of the task. There is some use of linking words to connect ideas within sentences, *but*; *also*; *if*; *though*, and the paragraphs are linked with cohesive devices, *However*; *Even*; *In my opinion*; *In conclusion*.
Language	5	There is a range of everyday, topic-specific vocabulary used appropriately, *purchasing*; *process of shopping*; *boring*; *fashionable*; *queues*; *enormous*; *amusing*. There are also some examples of some less common phrases, *a terrible waste of time*; *comparing sales*. There is a range of simple and some more complex grammatical structures used with a good degree of control, *It helps me to decide*; *don't entertain me at all if they have*, and although the final sentence has an error, the meaning is still clear, *would be more entertaining if they will be improved*. There are some errors with word order, *where can I save*; *seems me to be*, but these do not impede.

Sample answer B

> I like too much shopping, I like searching new things and clothes with some friends of mine or my boyfriend. I go with them every week-end in Novara to my favourite shops. But some of them are too expensive for me and for normal people, so, if I want to buy something that I like, I can't, because of the prices. I think that shopping centres could do more sales, so, there will go more persons to buy, or they could create an innovative shop (different to the others) for attract people. I hope that people think the same!

Subscale	Mark	Commentary
Content	5	All content is relevant to the task. The target reader is fully informed as all questions in the task have been covered.
Communicative Achievement	3	The text is written using an appropriate style and register for an article. There is language of personal opinion and suggestion which is used to communicate straightforward ideas.
Organisation	3	Although the text only contains one paragraph, the ideas are connected and coherent through the use of linking words, *or*; *But*; *and*; *so*; *because*. There is also some use of simple cohesive devices, such as relative pronouns to avoid repetition of nouns, *them*; *there*; *they*; *think the same*.
Language	3	Everyday vocabulary related to the topic of shopping is used generally appropriately, *clothes*; *favourite shops*; *prices*; *sales*; *create an innovative shop*. The text is mainly written in the present tense, which is generally used correctly, and there are a few examples of simple modal verbs, *could do*; *will go*; *could create*, and a conditional, *if I want to buy something that I like, I can't, because of the prices*. There are a few minor errors with word order, *I like too much shopping*; *so there will go more persons*, but these do not impede communication.

Question 3

Sample answer A

> "...Jack climbed out of the boat and ran as fast as he could to the beach. He was followed by some little and dangerous sharks. When he finally got on the beach, he realized that he is on a abandonated island. The island wasn't too big - ; it was just around 650 kilometers in diameter. It was a tropic island with some coconut trees on it. Suddenly, he saw a boat that crashed on the island's beach. He immediatly ran there, and helped the boat's capitan. The capitan was a poor old lady. After Jack helped her to get out of the boat, the old lady sudenly died, because of the accident. Jack was freaked out, and he tried to build a boat from the coconut trees, to get back home..."

Subscale	Mark	Commentary
Content	5	All the content is relevant to the task. The target reader is fully informed as there is a clear connection between the story and the prompt sentence.
Communicative Achievement	5	The story continues from the prompt sentence in an appropriate style. There is some good use of narrative tenses and descriptive vocabulary, *dangerous sharks*; *tropic island*; *coconut trees*; *crashed*, which provide extra details and help to hold the reader's attention. Straightforward ideas are communicated and the story has a clear beginning, middle and an end.
Organisation	4	The story is generally well organised despite the fact that it only contains one paragraph. The use of the past tenses provides a structure to the text and cohesive devices link the events well, *He was followed by*; *When he finally*; *Suddenly*; *He immediately*; *After*. Some of the sentences are quite short, but this doesn't affect the structure of the story.
Language	4	There is some good use of everyday vocabulary linked to desert islands, *sharks*; *island*; *tropic*; *coconut*; *freaked out*, which help to describe the scene more clearly. There is a range of simple and some more complex grammatical forms used with a good degree of control. For example, *He was followed by*; *he finally got on*; *he realized*; *wasn't too big*; *he saw a boat that crashed*; *He immediatly ran there*; *he tried to build a boat*. There are some errors with tenses, *that he is on* and some punctuation slips, *coconut trees*, *to get back home*, but these do not impede.

Sample answer B

> Jack climbed out of the boat and ran as fast as he could to the beach. He ran without stop in the jungle but the pirates still ran to catch him.
>
> Jack arrived into a cave where he was hided. He stayed there for a few minutes. The pirates wasn't there when he came out from the cave.
>
> Jack was a pirate too so he was going back to the boat while the other pirates tried to find him in the jungle. Jack stole the pirates boat and their golds.
>
> Jack returned to his home with a boat of full gold.

Subscale	Mark	Commentary
Content	5	All the content is relevant to the task. The target reader is fully informed as there is a clear connection between the story and the prompt sentence.
Communicative Achievement	3	The story has a simple narrative with a clear beginning, middle and an end. There is some attempt to create suspense and excitement when describing the action, *he ran without stop*; *he was hided*; *Jack stole the pirates boat and their golds*, and straightforward ideas are communicated.
Organisation	3	Although the text is quite simple, there are some linking words, *but*; *so*, and some cohesive devices, *him*; *where*; *there*; *when*; *while*; *their*, which are used to connect the action of the story and to create a logical time sequence. The sentences all have a similar structure, each starting with Jack or *he* or *the pirates*, which makes the story slightly repetitive.
Language	3	The vocabulary is appropriate for the task and there are some interesting vocabulary choices, *jungle*; *pirates*; *cave*; *golds*, which help to create the story. The grammar is generally correct, although it is quite simple. The sentences are quite short and there is some good use of regular and irregular simple past verbs, *ran*; *arrived*; *stayed*; *came out*; *was*; *tried to find him*; *stole*; *returned*. There are a few errors with verb forms, *without stop*; *was hided*; *pirates wasn't there*, but these do not impede communication.

Listening

Part 1

1 B   **2** B   **3** A   **4** C   **5** A   **6** A   **7** B

Part 2

8 C   **9** A   **10** C   **11** A   **12** B   **13** C

Part 3

14 Brokley   **15** half past eight / eight thirty / 8.30   **16** blue   **17** receptionist
18 hall   **19** 3 / three

Part 4

20 A   **21** C   **22** B   **23** A   **24** C   **25** B

Further feedback available in the downloadable resources

Transcript

Test One. There are four parts to the test. You will hear each part twice. We will now stop for a moment. Please ask any questions now because you must not speak during the test.

PART 1	*Now look at the instructions for Part One.*
	For each question, choose the correct answer. Look at question one.
Question 1	*One. Where does the man think he left his wallet?*
Man:	Hello, my name's Joe Smith. I'm ringing because I lost my black leather wallet on Monday. I got off the eleven twenty train from Reading and went to the shop at the end of platform two. I bought some sandwiches so I had my wallet then. Afterwards <u>I went to sit in the waiting room. I remember putting my wallet down. I probably left it there</u> because my next train arrived, so I hurried off to get it. If it's handed in, please can you contact me on 07577886.
	Now listen again.
	[repeat]
Question 2	*Two. What is tomorrow's talk at the Nature Society about?*
Woman:	Do you fancy coming along to tomorrow's Nature Society talk?
Man:	Yeah, the last one on rivers and the plants around them was very good, wasn't it?
Woman:	Well, you'll like the next topic too. It's something you're interested in.
Man:	Ah – so it's about rainforests then?
Woman:	I knew you'd think that – actually there's a talk on that next month. This one'll deal with something closer to home – <u>wild flowers in parks and gardens</u>.
Man:	Oh, OK. Not as interesting as jungle wildlife but it still sounds worth going to.
	Now listen again.
	[repeat]
Question 3	*Three. What will the woman order for lunch?*
Woman:	The menu looks good, doesn't it?
Man:	Yes. Have you decided what you're going to order? <u>You normally have salad for lunch</u>, don't you?
Woman:	Yes, I was thinking I might have the tomato soup, or maybe a toasted cheese and tomato sandwich. They both sound nice and I've heard the bread here's really good. They bake it themselves.
Man:	Look, it says everything on the lunchtime menu comes with fresh bread.

	Woman:	In that case, <u>I'll go for my usual choice</u>.
	Man:	OK, well, I'm going to try the soup.

Now listen again.

[repeat]

Question 4 *Four. How did the woman find out about the exhibition?*

Woman: Hi Jack. Did you know there's an interesting new exhibition on at the local art gallery? I was looking at the gallery's website recently and I didn't see anything about it. I'm surprised they haven't advertised it more on posters around town either. Anyway, <u>according to what I heard on the radio</u>, it's only on for a couple of days and I think it'll be really popular. I can book tickets online, if you're interested. Let me know as soon as you can.

Now listen again.

[repeat]

Question 5 *Five. What job is the woman's brother doing?*

Woman: Did I tell you my brother's working at Scooter – that new designer clothes place in town? You know, the one that sells really original jeans and T-shirts?

Man: I'm quite jealous! I'd like to work there as a shop assistant myself.

Woman: Well, in fact, he wanted to do that, but <u>they only needed a security guard for the shop. So he was given that job instead</u>. He's pleased – and he gets a great discount on all those amazing designer clothes!

Man: Cool!

Now listen again.

[repeat]

Question 6 *Six. How will the woman travel to her meeting?*

Woman: Hi Brian. This is Amanda, Amanda Smith. I'm calling to let you know that I might be a little late for our meeting. They've cancelled my train. It's really annoying actually as the train's the fastest way to get into town. I tried to get a cab, but the queue at the station was so long. <u>It'll be quicker to rush home and get my own car</u> rather than wait for a taxi. So I'll see you soon, hopefully.

Now listen again.

[repeat]

Question 7 *Seven. Which sport has the man stopped doing?*

Woman: You're doing lots of winter sports this year, aren't you?

Man: That's right. Snow-boarding's been a first-time experience for me. It's taken me a while to learn, but now I find it hard to stop!

Woman: What else have you tried?

Man: <u>Ice-hockey</u> too – I've always enjoyed watching it. It's too fast, though, and <u>I gave it up in the end</u>. Skiing's a bit scary but it's so exciting that I just can't get enough of it. It's a shame it's such an expensive sport to do.

Woman: Yes, I know.

Now listen again.

[repeat]

That is the end of Part One.

PART 2   *Now look at Part Two.*

For each question, choose the correct answer.

Question 8   *Eight. You will hear two people talking about buying a bicycle.*

Woman: So have you bought a bicycle yet?

Man: I nearly bought one last week – but in the end I didn't really think the salesman I spoke to knew enough.

Woman: In our local bike shop? They're usually very helpful in there.

Man: Yes. I think he was new. Anyway, maybe I need to do some more research online.

Woman: If you look on the internet, sometimes there's too much information. <u>What about talking to my brother who's a professional cyclist</u>? He'd give you some useful ideas without trying to persuade you to buy a particular product like they do in shops.

Man: I could do.

Now listen again.

[repeat]

Question 9   *Nine. You will hear a man telling his friend about his Welsh language course.*

Woman: How are you getting on with your Welsh language course?

Man: Not too bad actually. From what other people had told me, I thought the grammar would be really hard, but actually it isn't too bad. The main issue I have to deal with is <u>our teacher – if she spoke more slowly, I'd understand a lot more</u>. I miss so much. Oh well, I'm sure I'll get used to her. Our classes are only an hour long though, so just when I'm getting into the lesson, it's over! Anyway, it's a beautiful language and I'm glad I've taken it up.

Now listen again.

[repeat]

Question 10   *Ten. You will hear a woman telling her colleague about her weekend.*

Man: Morning! So how was your weekend?

Woman: We went to the city for the day, to the new outdoor street market everyone's talking about. It never stopped raining though and we all got very wet. I was happy to leave. Both the kids spent the next day coughing the whole time. <u>That meant we just sat on the sofa watching TV all afternoon, which was something I really needed to do</u>, despite all the arguments about what to watch. We did eventually manage to find a couple of films that everyone would be satisfied with.

Now listen again.

[repeat]

Question 11   *Eleven. You will hear two friends talking about a new restaurant.*

Man: Have you been to the new restaurant on the High Street?

Woman: Yes, I guess it wasn't too bad.

Man: I thought the food was pretty good value at least.

Woman: It's true they don't charge too much.

Man: The service was slow though when I went. The waiter had to apologise.

Woman: I don't mind waiting when the food's all freshly cooked. But it was quick enough when I went. That was just it – <u>everything seemed to either be out of a tin or frozen stuff heated up in a microwave</u>.

Man: <u>Such a shame, but you're absolutely right</u> – even if it isn't an expensive place to eat.

Now listen again.

[repeat]

Question 12   *Twelve. You will hear two old friends talking at a party.*

Woman: Oh hi, John, it is you! I thought so – I'd recognise that jacket anywhere.

Man: You know it's always been my favourite.

Woman: Yes, but I thought you'd have a new one after all these years!

Man: Why bother, if it still fits as well as ever? After all, fashion has never interested me that much. I see you have to wear glasses now as well. I'm still not really used to mine.

Woman: But they look good on you, particularly now you've shaved your beard.

Man: Thanks. Anyway, what have you been doing since I last saw you? You look well.

Now listen again.

[repeat]

Question 13   *Thirteen. You will hear two colleagues talking about a meeting.*

Man: Where's this afternoon's meeting?

Woman: Well it was supposed to be upstairs, but surely we're not going to have it now that John's off sick?

Man: Oh? I've heard we're going to carry on as planned.

Woman: I can't believe that. Without John? Oh well, I'm ready for it … I'm doing my presentation and I think everyone'll like it.

Man: I'm sure you'll be great! Did it take long to prepare?

Woman: To be honest, I spent ages on it. That was fine, but my laptop kept shutting down while I was preparing it. That made me really mad!

Man: Oh dear!

Now listen again.

[repeat]

That is the end of Part Two.

PART 3   *Now look at Part Three.*

For each question, write the correct answer in the gap. Write one or two words or a number or a date or a time.

Look at questions 14 to 19 now. You have 20 seconds.

You will hear a man giving information to people who are starting a one-week singing course.

Man: Hello, everyone. I'm delighted you've chosen to do this one-week singing course. Before we start, I'll give you some important information.

First of all, your teachers. As you know, we're running classes in two different singing styles and each has its own teacher. The jazz course will be taught by Robert Park – some of you will remember him from last year. And Susan Brokley will teach you to sing songs from famous musicals. Her surname's spelt B-R-O-K-L-E-Y.

The course highlight is the concert for family and friends on Friday. It'll begin at half past eight, but if your guests want to get the best seats to watch you, theatre doors open at eight o'clock.

On the night of the concert, we want you to feel relaxed – T-shirts are fine – but we ask that they're blue so everyone looks similar. The traditional colour for concerts is black, of course, but we think that's a bit dark. You'll enjoy performing I'm sure.

Now for some other information. To find your way around the building, you can always ask your teachers or the security guard, if you need help. There's also a map showing where all the rooms are, which you can get from the receptionist. I'll introduce you in a moment.

The lunch break will be at 1pm! We don't have a café, I'm afraid. There's a kitchen for preparing food, but there's nowhere to sit and eat there. So, take your sandwiches or whatever to the hall – much nicer, with a view of the garden next door.

If anyone's using the public car park, there's a charge. A monthly pass costs £20. As you're only here for a week, it's cheaper to <u>pay daily, which is £3</u>, so that'll only cost you £15 in total. OK?

So, any questions?

Now listen again.

[repeat]

That is the end of Part Three.

PART 4 *Now look at Part Four.*

For each question, choose the correct answer. Look at questions 20 to 25 now. You have 45 seconds.

You will hear an interview with a man called Mickey Diaz, who is talking about his work as a hairdresser.

Woman: Welcome to the careers interview. Today we're talking to Mickey Diaz who'll tell us what it's like to work as a hairdresser. Mickey, why did you become a hairdresser?

Man: Both my parents were hairdressers and worked with lots of well-known TV stars but I really expected to do something completely different. It was after college when I was looking for work that a <u>friend said I could help in his hairdresser's shop</u>, so I did, and I ended up staying!

Woman: So, what's a normal working day like?

Man: Busy! I get in early. We decide who's going to do which jobs each day – <u>it's best if we mix things up</u> – do a few women's cuts, some mens, some colour. Stopping for a coffee or a rest can be difficult but I always make time for that. I often stay late to prepare things for the next day too, but that's fine with me.

Woman: What's the best part of the job?

Man: <u>I really enjoy exchanging news with the people who come back regularly for haircuts.</u> Sometimes they want a new style and ask me to be creative. I'm not keen on doing that – I prefer to show people pictures of the latest haircuts and get them to choose one instead.

Woman: So, is there anything you don't like about your job?

Man: Some hairdressers get upset if customers are rude, but I never let anyone bother me. We have to take <u>health and safety courses which I find extremely dull</u> but I know they're necessary. I'm also responsible for training new colleagues at the shop. I prefer cutting hair – I don't mind sharing my knowledge though.

Woman: I see. How does it feel when you've finished a haircut?

Man: It's very important to me to get a haircut right but when the customer walks out of the door, the hair's already growing back. I know I won't see that exact same cut again, which is a shame. I usually feel there's something I could do better, so <u>I'm always trying to improve</u>, to keep customers satisfied.

Woman: Finally, any advice for people who'd like to become hairdressers?

Man: You can study hairdressing at college, but you don't learn as much as you would in a full-time job. People often think hairdressing's badly paid but the money can actually be quite good with tips added. Never forget that you're only as good as your last haircut – <u>a lot of people make the mistake of thinking they've learned all there is to learn – that's rarely true.</u>

Woman: Well, Mickey…(fade)

Now listen again.

[repeat]

That is the end of Part Four.

You now have six minutes to write your answers on the answer sheet.

You have one more minute.

That is the end of the test.

Test 2 answer key

Reading

Further feedback available in the downloadable resources

Part 1

1 A   **2** C   **3** B   **4** A   **5** B

Part 2

6 B   **7** E   **8** F   **9** C   **10** H

Part 3

11 C   **12** A   **13** B   **14** D   **15** B

Part 4

16 C   **17** F   **18** D   **19** G   **20** B

Part 5

21 C   **22** D   **23** A   **24** B   **25** A   **26** D

Part 6

27 be   **28** with   **29** of   **30** us   **31** to   **32** than

Writing

Question 1

Sample answer A

Hello Robbie

Thank you for your email! I'm so glad that you will celebrate your birthday in a restuarant. I think it's a really cool idea, because it will be a really memorible birthday.

Also about the restuarants. I recomend the we should go in a burger restuarant, because everyone loves burgers and fastfood. It will be grateful if you will pick me up to the restuarant. My parents are always at work, so I don't think they can take me to the restuarant.

Also I've got a question to ask you. Should we go to the restuarant in street clothes or we all need to be properly dressed? I hope you will answer me soone.

Your friend

Dima

Subscale	Mark	Commentary
Content	5	All content is relevant to the task. The target reader is fully informed about the four points in the task.
Communicative Achievement	5	The email is written in a consistently friendly tone, using the conventions of an informal email, *Hello Robbie*; *Thank you for your email*; *it's a really cool idea*; *everyone loves burgers*; *I hope you will answer me soone*; *your friend*. There is a range of functional language used, agreeing, expressing opinions, making requests and asking questions, all of which help to hold the reader's attention and communicate straightforward ideas.
Organisation	5	The text is organised into paragraphs and the ideas are linked logically and coherently through the use of linking words, *because*; *Also*; *so*; *or*. Each separate idea is clearly introduced and expanded through the use of cohesive devices, *about the restuarants. I recomend the we should go…*; *My parents are always at work, so I don't think…*; *I've got a question to ask you. Should we…* The length of the sentences, often consisting of two clauses, improves the overall cohesion of the text. The punctuation is generally accurate, but there are a few slips.
Language	5	There is a range of everyday vocabulary which is suitable for the task, *celebrate*; *cool*; *fastfood*; *grateful*; *properly dressed*, and an attempt at some less common vocabulary, *memorible*. There is a range of simple and some more complex grammatical forms, particularly in the way the sentences are constructed, *I think it's a really cool idea, because it will be*; *My parents are always at work, so I don't think they can take me.* There are some errors with spelling, *restuarant*; *soone*, but other errors are due to ambition, *recomend the we should go*; *pick me up to the restaurant*; *or we all need to be*.

Sample answer B

> Hello First I want to wish you a happy birthday! And thanks for the invitation, I would love to come. I think its a really good idea to have more people, because with more people there will be more fun, plus people can meet each other and make new friends.
>
> Personaly I think you should host the party in the first restourant, people will have a wider range of options, plus there might be a vegan menu
>
> Thanks for asking I would like for you to pick me up, because I don't have a car.
>
> And one more thing. Can you tell me if I have to dress specificly for the party?
>
> Daniel

Subscale	Mark	Commentary
Content	5	All content is relevant to the task. The target reader is fully informed about the four points in the task.
Communicative Achievement	3	The email is written in a generally appropriate style and register. There is a friendly tone, *Hello*; *thanks for the invitation*; *Can you tell me*, but there are also some more formal expressions, *plus*; *Personaly*; *a wider range of options*; *And one more thing*. Straightforward ideas are communicated and where opinions have been given, reasons have been provided to support the writer's views, *I think you should host the party in the first restaurant, people will have a wider range of options*.
Organisation	3	The text is connected and coherent and paragraphs have been used to separate the four points in the task. Some simple linking words have been used to link sentences, *And*; *because*; *plus*, but these are repeated through the text rather than using alternative cohesive devices. Some of the sentence punctuation is not always correct, *happy birthday! And thanks*; *asking I would like*. There are some direct references to the input material, *the first restaurant*; *Thanks for asking*, which are fine because there is some support which follows, *vegan menu*; *I don't have a car*. Without this support, it could be difficult to follow the text.
Language	3	There is a range of everyday language which is used appropriately for the task, *invitation*; *more fun*; *meet each other*; *host*; *options*; *vegan*. Simple grammar, including modal verbs, is used with a good degree of control, *I would love to come*; *with more people, there will be more fun*; *people will have*; *there might be*; *Can you tell me if I have to dress*. There some minor errors with spelling, *Personaly*; *restaurant*; *specificly*, but these do not impede.

Question 2

Sample answer A

> People in my age often go in the cinema or theater, make a picknick in our beautiful park or go in the sport centre. Unfortunately, most people also sitting in their hause and play computer games. This is a shack.
>
> I really enjoy organised any activities! I've got a lots of ideas for trips or games and my friends are always satisfied with my plans.
>
> I would like to try new laser game in our city. I like paintball and this is a very similar but it doesn't paintfull as paintball. I think it will be great!

Subscale	Mark	Commentary
Content	5	All content is relevant to the task. The target reader is fully informed as details have been given about all questions in the task.
Communicative Achievement	4	The text has been written in an appropriate article style. The tone is neutral but informative and personal opinions have been included, *People in my age often go*; *most people also sitting*; *I really enjoy*; *I would like to try*; *I think it will be great*. The text holds the reader's attention due to the details included, *make a picknick in our beautiful park*, but the errors sometimes make the reader struggle to understand what is being communicated, *This is a shack*; *it doesn't paintfull as paintball*.
Organisation	4	The text is generally well-organised. There are clear paragraphs and each one focuses on one of the aspects in the task. The ideas are expanded and linked through the use of linking words, *or*; *also*; *and*; *but*, and some cohesive devices, such as relative pronouns, *their*; *This*; *this*; *it*. There is also some attempt to contrast ideas using cohesive devices, such as *Unfortunately*, and in the final sentence, *this is a very similar but it…*
Language	3	Everyday vocabulary, linked to activities, is used appropriately, *cinema*; *theater*; *picknick*; *park*; *sport centre*; *computer games*; *trips*; *games*; *plans*; *laser game*; *paintball*. The grammatical structures are quite simple, mainly limited to present tenses, although there are a few examples of more complex tenses, *are always satisfied*; *would like to try*; *it will be*. There are some prepositions which have been used incorrectly, *in my age*; *go in the*, and there are some more noticeable errors, *most people also sitting in their hause*; *shack*; *organised any activities*; *a lots of*; *it doesn't paintful*, but the ideas are still communicated.

Sample answer B

> There are many activities that teens (10–13) can do in their free time in Shah
> Alam. The common activities that many people do is swimming, cinema or dancing.
> I enjoy taking part in organised activities because it's fun! However, I would like some
> new activities that young teens can do in Shah Alam. My ideas are: rollerblading,
> skateboarding, benchball, photography, dodgeball, Art & Craft, sewing and cooking.
> All of those activities are available to both girls and boys.

Subscale	Mark	Commentary
Content	5	All content is relevant to the task. The target reader is fully informed as details have been given about all the questions in the task.
Communicative Achievement	3	The text has been written using an informal tone and the writer has expressed their own opinion, *I enjoy…because it's fun*, and given some details about the activities young people can do, *swimming*, *cinema or dancing*. However, there is a lack of detail and the points are not expanded to include extra information, which would interest the reader. For example in the second point, although they say they like taking part in organised activities, they don't provide details of what they are.
Organisation	3	The text is logical and follows the structure of the input material. There is some use of linking words to connect the ideas, *or*; *because*; *and*, and different words are used to avoid repetition, *There are many activities*; *The common activities*. However, there is a limited use of cohesive devices, *However*; *those*, and the information is often presented in a list format, *rollerblading, skateboarding, benchball, photography, dodgeball, Art & Craft, sewing and cooking*, with no extra information provided.
Language	3	There is some appropriate vocabulary used related to the topic of activities, *swimming, cinema or dancing*; *rollerblading, skateboarding, benchball, photography, dodgeball, Art & Craft, sewing and cooking*. In terms of grammatical structures, the language is quite simple, mainly using the present tense, and often repeating the language in the input material, *that teens can do*; *I enjoy taking part…*; *I would like some new activities*; *are available*. There are very few errors and these do not impede communication, *activities that many people do is*.

Question 3

Sample answer A

> As I came out of the supermarket, I saw someone that I had wanted to see for a long
> time. It was my friend Viktor. We were going to same school. After we graduated from
> school each one of us chose different universities When I saw him I got close to him and
> he also saw me. We greeted each other and started a conversation. "Now I am studying
> meteorology in Kral Federal University. For now, I think it is interesting" I said. "Well, if I
> need a weather forecast I will call you. By the way, right now I am not studying. Instead
> of that I help my parents with family buisness". After nice conversation we arranged to
> meet an weekend and I walked away."

Subscale	Mark	Commentary
Content	5	All content is relevant to the task. The target reader is fully informed as the story follows on logically from the prompt sentence.
Communicative Achievement	4	This story shows some of the conventions used in story writing, such as introducing new characters, direct speech and a clear narrative sequence. There is some background information, *After we graduated from school each one of us chose different universities*, and an idea that the story will continue, *we arranged to meet an weekend and I walked away.* The ideas are not very complicated, but the reader's attention is held due to the interaction between the characters.
Organisation	4	The text is generally well-organised. There is a range of tenses and some cohesive devices connected with time, which provide a clear narrative sequence, *After we graduated from school*; *When I saw him*; *We greeted each other and started*; *I am studying*; *it is interesting*; *I help my parents*; *After...we arranged to meet...and I walked away.* Other cohesive devices are also used to link the ideas within the sentences, *Well*; *By the way*; *Instead of that*.
Language	4	There is a range of everyday vocabulary, which is suitable for the task, used appropriately, *graduated*; *universities*; *greeted*; *conversation*; *meteorology*; *weather forecast*. The past tenses are generally used to good effect and there are other grammatical forms used with a good degree of control, *if I need a weather forecast I will call you. I am not studying. Instead of that I help; we arranged to meet'*. There are some minor errors, *We were going; each one of us; I got close to him; an weekend*, but these do not affect communication.

Sample answer B

As I cam out the supermarkets, I saw someone that I had wanted to see for a long time. It was my ex-girlfriend. I said hello to her and we handed with each other. She and me went to a cafe where we have been there and chatted together. She said she had been married for 3 years. She didn't work. She worked at home and had 2 babies. I said: "It's very good. How happy with you!" She said: "Thank you." We also talked about that we were together. It was a nice memory. I won't forget forever. She very thankful to me. She said I was the best ex-boyfriend. I also talked to her about the experience about these fears. After thant, I drive her to the home. In the car, she said "I missed you." I said "I missed you, too. But, time is changed everything. We back to that time any more."

Subscale	Mark	Commentary
Content	5	All content is relevant to the task. The target reader is fully informed as the story follows on logically from the prompt sentence.
Communicative Achievement	4	The text uses some features of story writing. There is a clear narrative, and a new character is introduced. There is some direct speech and the story has a clear conclusion. The reader's attention is held due the relationship between the characters and the emotional content which appears at the end, *In the car, she said "I missed you." I said "I missed you, too. But, time is changed everything"*.
Organisation	3	The text is connected and coherent and there is some attempt to organise the information with a range of narrative tenses, *She said she had been married for 3 years. She didn't work; We also talked about that we were together.* Many of the sentences are quite short and are connected through the dialogue and a change in speaker, *I said...She said*, but there is some use of simple cohesive devices, such as relative pronouns and time phrases, *It; her; where; After than*.
Language	3	Everyday vocabulary is used generally appropriately, although there is some repetition, *she; said; talked.* The sentence structures are quite simple, often following the same pattern and generally starting with *she* or *I.* There is some accurate use of past tenses, *went to a cafe; she had been married; worked at home and had; we were together,* but there are also some errors, *where we have been there; she very thankful; time is changed everything.* There are phrases which although they can generally be understood, are not accurate, *we handed with each other; How happy with you; forget forever; the experience about these fears; We back to that time any more.*

Listening

Part 1

1 A   **2** C   **3** B   **4** A   **5** A   **6** A   **7** C

Part 2

8 B   **9** A   **10** B   **11** C   **12** B   **13** A

Part 3

14 art   **15** people   **16** animals   **17** acting   **18** eight / 8 months   **19** website

Part 4

20 B   **21** C   **22** A   **23** C   **24** A   **25** B

Transcript

Test Two. There are four parts to the test. You will hear each part twice. We will now stop for a moment. Please ask any questions now, because you must not speak during the test.

PART 1	*Now look at the instructions for Part One.*
	For each question, choose the correct answer. Look at question one.

Question 1	*One. What has the man forgotten to pack for the trip?*
Woman:	Hi Freddy! All ready for the camping trip? Your backpack looks very full.
Man:	Well, I didn't want to forget my sleeping bag like the last time I went camping. I was lucky then and it wasn't too cold. I hope I've remembered everything this time.
Woman:	Well, so long as you've got your sleeping bag, plus a torch and walking boots, you'll be fine.
Man:	Oh dear. <u>I've just realised I've left my torch behind</u>. At least I've got my walking boots. Never mind I'll probably manage.
Woman:	You'll be fine.

Now listen again.

[repeat]

Question 2	*Two. What time is the plane expected to depart?*
Man:	This is an announcement for all passengers waiting to travel on the 10.45 flight to Glasgow. Due to poor weather, <u>this flight is delayed and is unlikely to take off until 12.15</u>. All passengers travelling on this flight can collect a special ticket at the information desk, which they can exchange for a drink and a snack at the cafe. Please note the check-in desk will close at 11.30. We apologise for the delay to your flight and will give you further updates as soon as we can.

Now listen again.

[repeat]

Question 3	*Three. Where did the family go at the weekend*
Man:	How was your weekend? Were there any tickets left for the play you wanted to see?
Woman:	Yes, but we decided to do something else in the end. I found a few more options online. <u>We ended up getting some discount tickets to visit a castle</u>. We all enjoyed it far more than the art gallery we went to last time we had a family day out. We're actually thinking of going there again. It's just as much fun as going to see a show at the theatre.

Now listen again.

[repeat]

Question 4   *Four. What are the man and woman going to order?*

Man: What shall we have to drink? I'm quite thirsty, so I think I'll just have water.

Woman: Me, too. Let's get a large bottle to share.

Man: Yes, we could do that. Do you prefer sparkling? I always have still.

Woman: Oh, I like sparkling water. How about getting a glass of still and a glass of sparkling? (short pause) Actually, have you seen the prices? <u>What about asking for a jug of tap water</u> – it tastes just as good.

Man: Especially if they put ice and lemon in it. Good idea.

Now listen again.

[repeat]

Question 5   *Five. Which photograph did the man take?*

Woman: Your website's great. Did you take all these photos?

Man: Not all of them. I included some others that were taken by friends, like this one of the desert. You can tell which are mine because the style's different. <u>I'm interested in water, especially scenes showing rain. Have a look at this one of mine.</u>

Woman: Nice! And is this one yours? I love how the water in the lake's like a mirror for the trees.

Man: It's beautiful, isn't it? It's actually someone else's work though.

Now listen again.

[repeat]

Question 6   *Six. How does the man suggest his friends should travel to the concert?*

Man: Hi, it's Neil. Listen, I know I was supposed to give you and Jack a lift to the concert tonight in my car but I'm not going to be able to make it. It's a shame my ticket'll be wasted. Anyway, it's not that far to the concert hall from where you both live. <u>You could always take the underground to Greenoaks station</u> and it's only a short walk from there. I'm sure you and Jack'll be able to take a taxi home afterwards? Anyway, I hope you both have fun. Bye!

Now listen again.

[repeat]

Question 7   *Seven. What is the weather forecast for the north this morning?*

Woman: Now for an update on the weather. Well, it's looking very different from yesterday in both the north and the south. In southern areas, there'll be some thick fog to begin with, making conditions difficult for people driving to work. That should disappear by around eleven, though. <u>There'll be heavy snow showers, mainly in northern areas,</u> but hopefully these will be over by lunchtime. It'll be calm everywhere for most of the day, but with some strong winds coming in towards the evening.

Now listen again.

[repeat]

That is the end of Part One.

PART 2   *Now look at Part Two. For each question, choose the correct answer.*

Question 8   *Eight. You will hear a boy telling a friend about plans for his birthday.*

Woman: What are you doing for your birthday?

Boy: I'm having a group bike ride and then a picnic in the park. I know it's the same as what we did last year but I don't think that matters. I wanted to have all my mates from college and my football team. But <u>it wouldn't be a good idea to have so many people riding together, so I'll have to choose between them, which is a shame.</u>

Woman: I'm sure it'll be fun whoever comes.

Boy: You're right. I hate having to make decisions like this. Anyway, you'll come, won't you?

Woman: Of course!

Now listen again.

[repeat]

Question 9 *Nine. You will hear two friends talking about a football match they went to.*

Man: Did you enjoy the match last night? I have to say I thought it was pretty dull.

Woman: Oh I don't know – most people seemed to be enjoying it. Me included. <u>Although there weren't nearly as many people watching as there normally are.</u>

Man: <u>The cold weather might be the reason for the low numbers.</u> And the people who were there weren't too happy with some of the things the referee did.

Woman: He had some difficult situations to deal with. I didn't think he did too badly actually.

Man: Anyway, at least our team won. That's what matters!

Now listen again.

[repeat]

Question 10 *Ten. You will hear a man telling his friend about a skiing holiday.*

Man: I'm never going skiing again!

Woman: Why? You looked like you were having a good time in the photos I saw on the internet.

Man: They were taken at the start of the holiday. I was so excited then.

Woman: So, what happened?

Man: Everything was fine until someone suggested trying one of the more advanced routes. I've never been so scared in all my life. It was too difficult for me and I had to give up half-way – I nearly hurt myself hitting a tree! <u>The others all found this very funny, which made me feel pretty silly.</u>

Woman: Oh dear.

Now listen again.

[repeat]

Question 11 *Eleven. You will hear two friends talking about cars.*

Man: I hear you just bought a new car. How did you decide which one to get?

Woman: Well, I often watch that TV show about cars … you know the one with Ben Clark where they give all sorts of information about different models. <u>They mentioned some useful places to look online where people who've bought new cars give their opinions.</u> I'd always rather see what car owners say than trust adverts or stuff on TV. Anyway, they were all pretty positive about the model I was hoping to get so I went for it in the end!

Now listen again.

[repeat]

Question 12 *Twelve. You will hear a woman telling a friend about a singing competition.*

Man: How are things going with preparations for the singing competition?

Woman: Well, there are some strong singers this year, so I'm glad picking the winner's not my job. I mean, how do you go about choosing?

Man:		Have you ever thought about entering a singing competition yourself?
Woman:		I think it's more fun watching and making comments about everyone else! And anyway, being in charge of the whole thing, <u>I've more than enough to do, I can tell you. I'm spending ages sorting things out, including most evenings</u>. But I love it.
Man:		I'm sure it'll be great.

Now listen again.

[repeat]

Question 13   *Thirteen. You will hear a woman talking to a friend about her recent move to a city.*

Man:	Are you happy about your move to the city?
Woman:	Well, my neighbours are very quiet but there's a lot of street noise from all the shops and restaurants. I suppose everything's nearby, so now I can walk everywhere, which means <u>I'm actually fitter than when I lived in the countryside. I hadn't expected that</u>. I do sometimes wonder whether this is the right area for me, but once I've got to know more people, I'll be able to decide if it's the sort of place I'm going to be happy in. Why don't you come round soon?
Man:	I'd love to.

Now listen again.

[repeat]

That is the end of Part Two.

PART 3   *Now look at Part Three.*

For each question, write the correct answer in the gap. Write one or two words or a number or a date or a time. Look at questions 14 to 19 now. You have 20 seconds.

You will hear a woman called Kelly Robinson talking about her work as a maker of cartoon films.

Woman: My name's Kelly Robinson and I make cartoons for a living. I do this on computers and I've been doing the job since I left university. Although I now know almost as much about computing as I do about cartoon design, I actually <u>studied art for my degree</u>.

I got a job with a major film studio soon after leaving university. It's a great company to work for. The software programmes we use for making cartoons are really good, <u>but it's the people there that make it such a fantastic place to work</u>.

Each department has its own special job to do when we're making a cartoon film. For example, <u>the one I'm in works on animals</u> in the story, while others focus on the human characters or the buildings. It's then the director's job to bring everything together.

I'm always learning new skills to help improve my work. I did a writing course last year and learnt a lot about different types of stories. And <u>I've just started doing acting classes</u>, which are surprisingly useful for understanding filmmaking, even though I don't plan to appear in any films.

Some companies make cartoons the old-fashioned way using thousands of individual drawings but this takes a long time. Using this technique, it can take about two years to create a full-length film. Compare that to the <u>eight months</u> it takes my company to do the same and you see the advantage of using computers.

My next cartoon project will be the first thing I've done that isn't a film for children. <u>It's actually something for a website</u>. After working on so many kids' comedies, it'll be an interesting challenge. (fade ...)

Now listen again.

[repeat]

That is the end of Part Three.

PART 4   *Now look at Part Four.*

For each question, choose the correct answer.

Look at questions 20 to 25 now. You have 45 seconds.

You will hear an interview with a girl called Rosie Banks, who swims in international competitions

Man:	This week, I'm joined by swimmer Rosie Banks, who swims in international competitions. Rosie, welcome. So, did you swim a lot when you were very young?
Girl:	Yes, before I even started school, my dad used to take <u>my brother Joel</u> and me to the pool in town. He just wanted us to do something in our free time that wasn't looking at a screen. Joel was better at swimming than anyone we knew, and I practised as often as possible <u>so I could swim as fast as him</u>.
Man:	And then you joined a swimming club and started training seriously?
Girl:	Yes, I was invited to join the club when I was 12. It took an hour to get to their pool. Mum drove me. We had to leave for training early each morning, but we enjoyed chatting on the journey. With all the training and competitions, <u>I couldn't attend school sometimes</u>, which I was unhappy about. I was always much busier than my friends, but I still met up with them when I had time.
Man:	And now you've had success at the Swim Stars International competition. Tell us about that.
Girl:	Well, I'd trained hard, and I expected to do well, although winning was still brilliant! Swimming isn't shown much on TV – it's usually famous footballers or tennis stars people love watching – so <u>I couldn't believe people wanted to read and watch interviews with me</u>!
Man:	So, I imagine it's expensive taking part in international competitions. Do you get help with the costs?
Girl:	Yes. Fortunately, a sportswear company pays for plane tickets, as long as I use their swimsuits, bags and other stuff showing their brand. <u>It'd be great if they also gave me financial support for hotels</u>, as my parents have to spend a lot on that kind of thing.
Man:	So, you've got a new swimming coach now. What changes has she made?
Girl:	Well, I'm doing the same regular fitness training. But, thanks to <u>her suggestions about the way I move my arms through the water</u>, I've already seen improvements in my speed. She's also looked at the food I eat – luckily she was satisfied with that. I'm very strict with my diet.
Man:	And you're going to Spain soon I hear.
Girl:	Well, I've got a short break first, and then I'm going on a special training course there for the whole summer. <u>I'll work with lots of swimmers I haven't met before</u>. I'm really looking forward to that. I won't do any races but it'll still be hard work.
Man:	Thanks Rosie….

Now listen again.

[repeat]

That is the end of Part Four.

You now have six minutes to write your answers on the answer sheet.

You have one more minute.

That is the end of the test.

Test 3 answer key

Reading

Further feedback available in the downloadable resources

Part 1

1 B   **2** A   **3** A   **4** A   **5** C

Part 2

6 F   **7** A   **8** H   **9** B   **10** D

Part 3

11 C   **12** B   **13** A   **14** B   **15** D

Part 4

16 E   **17** A   **18** D   **19** H   **20** B

Part 5

21 D   **22** B   **23** B   **24** D   **25** A   **26** C

Part 6

27 so   **28** every / each   **29** if / when(ever)   **30** why   **31** about   **32** There

Writing

Question 1

Sample answer A

Dear teacher,

I'm writing you to answer your last email. I think it's a good idea to invite a well known person, it will be better to invit a scientist because I'm very interesting in mathematics, science and biology. I would like to ask him what is the most difficult part of his job. I think to entertain the visitor after the talk, we must organize a litle reception with some food and col drink, some students will be able to take some photos with him.

I hope my email can help you.

Ama

Subscale	Mark	Commentary
Content	5	All content is relevant to the task. The target reader is fully informed about the four points in the task.
Communicative Achievement	5	The email is written using a formal register, which is appropriate for the task scenario of a student writing to a teacher. The tone is consistently polite, *Dear teacher*; *I think it's a good idea to*; *I hope my email can help you*, and there is language of suggestion and opinion, *it will be better to invit a scientist because*; *we must organize a litle reception*. The reader's attention is held and straightforward ideas are communicated.
Organisation	4	Although there are some long sentences which are punctuated with commas rather than separated by full stops, the letter is generally well-organised. The structure follows the order of the input material and refers back to it when addressing each point, *it's a good idea to invite a well known person*, *it will be better to*; *I would like to ask him*; *I think to entertain the visitor after the talk*. There are very few linking words used, *because*; *with*; *and*, but the text has a clear overall structure.
Language	4	Everyday vocabulary which is suitable for the task, is used appropriately, *mathematics*; *science*; *biology*; *reception*; *photos*. There is some range of tenses used and a good degree of control over some more complex structures, *it will be better to invit a scientist*; *what is the most difficult part of his job*; *we must organize a litle reception with some food*; *students will be able to take*. There are some errors, *invit*; *I'm very interesting*; *litle*; *col drink*, but these do not impede communication.

Sample answer B

Dear Miss Jones,

I hope you are well, I received your e-mail. I think that it will be better to invite a scientist because the last time we have been with an actor and also we can get new knowledge.

I would like to ask about how can we produce electrical energy with the recycable materials (glass, paper...) within spend a lot of money. I suggest that we can make a scientist fair and there we can show the easy ways to result our environment problems and safe our world as well show what we are studying.

Kind regards,

Gerson Smith

Subscale	Mark	Commentary
Content	5	All content is relevant to the task. The target reader is fully informed. Although there is no direct reference to the first point, the email is positive and the benefits of having a speaker are explained, *we can get new knowledge.*
Communicative Achievement	4	The email is written using an appropriate tone. The polite and semi-formal register is suitable for an email to a teacher from a student, *Dear Miss Jones; I hope you are well; Kind regards.* There are examples of functional language to express opinions and give reasons, *I think that it will be better; I suggest that we can make a scientist fair and there we can show...as well as show what we are studying,* and the reader would consider the information in the email.
Organisation	3	The email is connected and coherent, despite a few punctuation slips, *I hope you are well, I received your e-mail.* There are instances where the long sentences would benefit from commas to separate some of the information, for example the final sentence. There are examples of a few linking words and simple cohesive devices used to connect the ideas through the text, *because; the last time; also; and; as well,* and the paragraphs work well.
Language	3	Everyday vocabulary related to school, science and the environment is used appropriately, *knowledge; produce electrical energy; materials; scientist fair; environment problems; studying.* There is an attempt to use a range of grammatical forms, but these are not always successful due to word choices or incomplete ideas, *I received your e-mail; we have been with an actor and also we can get; within spend a lot; the easy ways to result our environment problems and safe our world as well show.* Some of the errors are examples of more complex structures having been attempted, rather than more simple ones.

Question 2

Sample answer A

> Computer games are a common free-time activity that most teenagers enjoy doing. I personally don't like them, but most of my friends love them. For me, they are a waste of time. They can seriosly damage a persons eyesight and make it anti-sociable, of course if that person spends too much time playing them. But, they also have positive sites. Computer games are great way of having stronger reflexes. For people from a non-English speaking countries they help them learn English more fastly, because most computer games are in English. Overall, computer games are a part of today's world and we should accept them as a free-time activity.

Subscale	Mark	Commentary
Content	5	All content is relevant to the task. The target reader is fully informed about all the points in the task.
Communicative Achievement	5	The article is written in an appropriately informative tone, and a neutral register is used consistently through the text. There is a good mix of personal and general information, *I personally don't like them*; *For me, they are*; *Computer games are a great way of having*; *For people from a non-English speaking countries*, and the ideas in the article are well balanced between positive and negative views. The reader's attention is held with ease.
Organisation	5	The text is generally well organised and although there is only one paragraph, the ideas are clearly linked and connected. The text is cohesive due to the structured way the ideas have been organised, moving from personal ideas to general ones, and concluding with a general overview. There is a variety of linking words and cohesive devices including relative pronouns and comparative structures, *I personally…but most of my*; *them*; *They*; *and*; *that person*; *But they also have*; *they help them*; *because*; *Overall*.
Language	4	Everyday vocabulary which is suitable for the topic of computer games and related issues is used appropriately, *free-time*; *waste of time*; *damage*; *eyesight*; *stronger reflexes*. There is a variety of sentence patterns and some good control of some more complex grammatical structures, *most teenagers enjoy doing*; *They can seriosly damage a persons eyesight*; *are a great way of having*; *we should accept them as*. There are some errors, but these are often due to attempting more complex language, *and make it anti-sociable*; *positive sites*, and the meaning is still communicated.

Sample answer B

> Playing computer games is so popular thouse days. My friends are enjoying playing computer games, so and I.
>
> The good things about playing computer games is that with playing your concentracion and logic is improving. Alsou you have good fun with your friends.
>
> The bad things is that playing computer games people waist they time insted to do something more usefull. Also siting in fron of computer damages the eyes.
>
> At the end there are more bad things about computer games becouse your bodye become more lazye seating front of the computer and your eyes a damaging.

Subscale	Mark	Commentary
Content	5	All content is relevant to the task. The target reader is fully informed about all points in the task.
Communicative Achievement	3	The article has been written in an appropriate style for a magazine. The positives and negatives of playing computer games are clearly described, *The good things*; *The bad things*, and personal opinions are given in the conclusion, *there are more bad things about computer games*. The article communicates straightforward ideas, which are easily understood by the reader.
Organisation	3	The article has a coherent structure due to the paragraphs which use simple cohesive devices to clearly introduce the different aspects of the task, *Playing computer games*; *The good things*; *The bad things*; *At the end*. Although the sentences are quite simple, they are connected with simple linking words, *and*; *Also*; *becouse*. However, they are not always successful, *so and I*; *Alsou*.
Language	3	Everyday vocabulary linked with computer games and health is used generally appropriately, *popular*; *concentracion*; *logic*; *improving*; *good fun*; *damages the eyes*. Simple grammatical forms, such as the present tenses are used with a good degree of control, *Playing computer games is so popular*; *My friends are enjoying playing*; *with playing your concentracion and logic is improving*; *there are more bad things about computer games*. The errors, mainly spelling, are noticeable, but they do not impede communication, *concentracion*; *Alsou*; *waist they time insted*; *usefull*; *siting in fron*; *becouse*; *bodye*; *lazye*.

Question 3

Sample answer A

It was my first time in the jungle and I was so excited. I have been always loved travelling, finally it has happend! Was I scared? No way!!! I was filled with desire to see all that animals, and birds, and plants that I saw in my books.

The most interesting meeting that day, was the collision with the monkey. We met her ocasionelly. She was sitting and feeding her baby, when we came into her territory. She looked at us, then she looked at her baby, and I had the felling that she understood, we didn't want to hurt her. Keeping silence, we stepped back to the jungle. It was amasing day!

Subscale	Mark	Commentary
Content	5	All content is relevant to the task. The target reader is fully informed as the story follows on logically from the prompt sentence.
Communicative Achievement	5	The story holds the reader's attention due to the use of short sentences in the first paragraph, *Was I scared? No way!!!*, and the description of the monkey in the second paragraph, *she looked at us, then she looked at her baby*. Straightforward ideas are communicated and the story has a clear beginning, middle and an end.
Organisation	5	The narrative has a clear sequence of events, which are linked with a variety of cohesive devices connected with time, *finally*; *that day*; *She was sitting… when we came*; *then*; *It was amasing day*. The use of commas isn't always accurate, *that day, was*; *baby, when*; *understood, we*, but the overall structure of the text and the variety of cohesive devices and linking words used is generally good.
Language	4	There is a range of everyday vocabulary connected to a jungle setting, *travelling*; *animals*; *birds*; *plants*; *monkey*; *territory*. There is an attempt to use a range of grammatical structures, *I was filled with desire to see*; *The most interesting meeting*; *She was sitting and feeding her baby, when we came*; *I had the felling that she understood*; *we stepped back*, but this is not always successful, *I have been always loved travelling*. There are a few errors, mainly with spelling, *happend*; *all that animals*; *ocasionelly*; *felling*; *keeping silence*; *amasing*, but these do not impede communication.

Sample answer B

> It was my first time the jungle and I was so excited. Let me tell you my story...
>
> Before we arrived at the airport close to the jungle, we met our guide. His name is Pete. When we landed, we instantly drove to our staying place. The second day we went to the jungle itself. We discovered a lot of animal shelters and brought a baby monkey back to their parents. After that, we went back 'home'. The last day was a little boring in the morning. That problem was solved by building a hut in the jungle. It was alot of fun. Then, we went back home.

Subscale	Mark	Commentary
Content	5	All content is relevant to the task. The target reader is fully informed as the story follows on logically from the prompt sentence.
Communicative Achievement	3	The story is a simple narrative which provides details of a trip to the jungle. There is some description of particular events, *we instantly drove*; *We discovered*; *building a hut*, and some explanation of how the characters felt, *was a little boring*; *It was alot of fun*. Straightforward ideas are presented in an appropriate story format.
Organisation	3	Despite the number of short sentences, the story is connected and coherent. There is a range of simple cohesive devices which help to sequence the narrative, *Before*; *When*; *The second day*; *After that*; *The last day*; *in the morning*; *Then, we went back home*, resulting in a clear story progression with a beginning, middle and an end.
Language	3	Everyday vocabulary relating to the jungle is used appropriately, *guide*; *animal shelters*; *monkey*; *building a hut*. The grammar is quite simple, but accurate, mainly using simple past tenses, *Before we arrived...we met*; *landed*; *drove*; *went*; *discovered*; *brought*; *was*; *was solved*. There are a few minor errors, *His name is Pete*; *staying place*; *their parents*; *a lot*, which do not impede communication.

Listening

Part 1

1 B   **2** C   **3** B   **4** B   **5** A   **6** C   **7** A

Part 2

8 B   **9** B   **10** C   **11** C   **12** B   **13** A

Part 3

14 8.15 / quarter past 8 / quarter past eight   **15** entrance   **16** palace
17 Wakizi   **18** diving   **19** sun(-)cream

Part 4

20 A   **21** B   **22** A   **23** B   **24** C   **25** C

> Further feedback available in the downloadable resources

Transcript

Test Three. There are four parts to the test. You will hear each part twice. We will now stop for a moment. Please ask any questions now, because you must not speak during the test.

PART 1   *Now look at the instructions for Part One*

For each question, choose the correct answer. Look at question one.

Question 1   *One. Why was the man late?*

Woman: What happened? I was getting worried.

Man: Sorry I'm so late. You know I've been having problems with my car. Well, it broke down completely last night so the bus was my only way of getting here, but it took ages.

Woman: Did the rain make the journey difficult?

Man: Actually that wasn't it. We were moving along quite fast until we got to the <u>traffic lights</u> in the town centre. I don't think they were working properly, and <u>there were long delays</u> before we got moving again.

Woman: Oh well, you're here now.

Now listen again.

[repeat]

Question 2   *Two. Why is the main road closed today?*

Woman: … and in today's local news, the main road in and out of town is closed so traffic is slow. It's best to avoid the area if you're driving. But if you're on foot, it's worth going to have a look at what's going on. <u>They're filming a movie, and people can come and watch</u>. There'll be a really good atmosphere in fact, just like the weekend when the charity bike race came through town. And remember, there's a street party next weekend, and the road will be closed for that too.

Now listen again.

[repeat]

Question 3   *Three. Where do they decide to have the wedding anniversary party?*

Man: Is there a plan yet for our grandparents' wedding anniversary party?

Woman: No, and it's their 50th anniversary so it has to be special.

Man: I thought about that smart new restaurant in town. It'd be perfect.

Woman: It's a bit far away, though.

Man: True. <u>We could always take them on a river cruise, and eat on board.</u>

Woman: <u>That's not a bad idea</u> ... I'll make the arrangements. It'd be better than having a garden party and inviting their friends over like we did last year.

Man: I'll leave it all to you then.

Now listen again.

[repeat]

Question 4   *Four. What does the man decide to order?*

Woman: Shall we have a look at the menu? What did you have last time?

Man: I had chicken and chips, but I think I'll have something different today. I was thinking about the pasta. What about you?

Woman: I fancy that too. <u>I had the pizza last time I came here</u> – it was delicious. I can really recommend it.

Man: Oh! <u>If it's as good as you say, I'll try it. I think I'd prefer that today actually.</u> Are you ready to order?

Woman: Yes, I know what I want. OK then. Let's order.

Now listen again.

[repeat]

Question 5   *Five. Which armchair is the man going to buy?*

Woman: What do you think of this armchair here?

Man: It looks really comfortable and I like the stripes, but I'm looking for one that will match the rest of my furniture.

Woman: <u>If I were you, I'd get this plain one, it's a nice size: not too big, not too small.</u>

Man: That's true. I like the look of the one over there, with the cushion, but it's too large for the space I have available.

Woman: So have you decided?

Man: <u>Yes, I'll go for the one you suggested.</u>

Now listen again.

[repeat]

Question 6   *Six. Which concert has the woman arranged to attend?*

Man: Are you planning to go to any of the concerts at the music festival next month?

Woman: Yeah, there's lots of good things on. You know <u>Billy Ryan the folk singer and guitar player? Well, I've got tickets for that.</u> Aren't you going to see the rock band Buzz?

Man: That's right.

Woman: I saw them recently – they're pretty good actually! Do you fancy seeing something together?

Man: There's a jazz band playing on the last day too. We could try that.

Woman: I'd rather get tickets for something else instead. I'll see what's available.

Now listen again.

[repeat]

Question 7   *Seven. Which tomatoes will the man use?*

Man: I'll start making the tomato sauce now. Can you pass me that knife?

Woman: Why don't you leave the tomatoes whole?

Man: The recipe says to cut them into slices. <u>I suppose these ones are small enough to use as they are though</u>.

Woman: <u>The sauce'll taste nicer like that</u>. Just cook them for a long time.

Man: I could just open a tin, you know. It'd be far easier.

Woman: That's cheating! You said you wanted to do this properly.

Man: <u>OK I'll follow your advice</u>.

Now listen again.

[repeat]

That is the end of Part One.

PART 2   *Now look at Part Two. For each question, choose the correct answer.*

Question 8   *Eight. You will hear two friends talking about doing exercise.*

Woman: Hi Tom, how are you?

Man: Fine thanks, but I need to get more exercise.

Woman: You could join a gym. The one at the end of your road's expensive, but it has lots of good machines.

Man: I know, but <u>it's when to go. I'm at work all day, often till late</u>. There's a swimming pool near my office, but it's always crowded there. The best option's probably cycling to work. Bikes cost a lot, so I guess I'll end up spending as much as I would on going to the gym, but I think I'll look for one anyway.

Now listen again.

[repeat]

Question 9   *Nine. You will hear two people talking in a restaurant.*

Man: What did you think of the meal? The soup had an unusual flavour.

Woman: I thought it needed more pepper and garlic. But <u>the salmon was wonderful</u>.

Man: It took a while to come, but <u>my tuna was gorgeous</u>. Lots of butter and herbs. I'd love to have the recipe. I'm not so sure about the dessert you had though – it looked a bit strange.

Woman: I thought it was really nice. In fact I'd say it was my favourite part of the meal. But unfortunately I couldn't eat it all.

Man: I'm not a fan of desserts. I'd rather have a bigger main dish.

Now listen again.

[repeat]

Question 10   *Ten. You will hear a woman telling her friend about her neighbours.*

Man: How are you getting on with your new neighbours?

Woman: Well, they always smile and say hello. I think they have a lot of visitors because I hear them chatting and playing music in the evenings.

Man: Oh, that's annoying, especially if you need to sleep!

Woman: Actually, I don't mind – I can sleep through anything, and they won't be able to complain if I make a noise! But <u>what bothers me is the mess they've left outside</u> – loads of empty boxes from when they moved in. I think I'll have a chat with them, but I don't want to seem rude.

Now listen again.

[repeat]

Question 11   *Eleven. You will hear two friends talking about a new museum.*

Woman: Have you been to the new history museum in the high street yet?

Man: Yes, it's fantastic, isn't it?

Woman: There was so much to see. The displays of 19th-century costumes were brilliant. I'm amazed you enjoyed looking at that kind of thing though, especially the fashion stuff … I really wanted to stay at the museum longer. It's a shame it closes so early. <u>Anyway, I wouldn't mind having another look around, but I'll have to wait until next weekend</u> as that's when I'm not working.

Now listen again.

[repeat]

Question 12   *Twelve. You will hear a man talking to a colleague about a hotel he stayed in.*

Woman: How was the hotel you stayed in?

Man: It was comfortable enough and easy to reach from the station, but <u>it wasn't walking distance from the city centre, which is how it was advertised</u>. It looked closer on the map. It was on a main road, so that was convenient for taxis, but there was lots of traffic. I was worried it'd be noisy in my room at night, but I hardly heard anything.

Woman: Would you recommend it for me and my husband?

Man: I was in a double room and there was only just enough space. Fine for me, but not really big enough for two.

Now listen again.

[repeat]

Question 13   *Thirteen. You will hear two passengers talking on an aeroplane.*

Man: We've finally taken off!

Woman: I'm so pleased. It's a while since I've flown, but I recently started a new job and the long distances I need to travel for it just <u>make flying a better option than the train</u>.

Man: I know what you mean. I do this same journey every month when I visit my family. They live a long way from the capital. I get nervous flying, but it's just so much easier than any other form of transport.

Woman: That's absolutely true, but I can never get comfortable in the seat. I like watching movies though to pass the time.

Now listen again.

[repeat]

That is the end of Part Two.

PART 3　　*Now look at Part Three*

For each question, write the correct answer in the gap. Write one or two words or a number or a date or a time. Look at questions 14 to 19 now. You have 20 seconds.

You will hear a tour guide talking about arrangements for a day trip to a place called Gulum.

Man:　　Good morning. You've all booked the trip to Gulum tomorrow, and I'd like to explain the arrangements for what will be a great day out. This is one of our most popular trips so you're sure to enjoy it.

We're meeting at eight o'clock in the morning as the <u>bus will go at exactly quarter past eight</u>. This is instead of the usual departure time of eight thirty. The reason for this is that, after picking you up, we've got to collect a number of passengers from other hotels. To get on the bus, please <u>meet at the entrance to the hotel</u> rather than at the reception desk, which gets quite crowded in the mornings.

So to the trip itself. Our first stop will be at a <u>magnificent ruin just outside Gulum. It used to be a palace</u>. I'm sure the guide mentioned it during the tour of the ancient theatre, if you went on that yesterday. The atmosphere there's really special, as you'll see for yourselves. Afterwards we'll drive on to the <u>Wakizi Restaurant</u> on the Gulum River for lunch. That's spelt W-A-K-I-Z-I, by the way – do check their menu online – it's fantastic! There'll be plenty of time to take photos while we're there.

In the afternoon, we'll stop at Gulum beach where there's a choice of activities to do. <u>One option is to go diving</u>. The variety of fish species on this part of the coast is quite amazing. For those people who like volleyball, we're organising a competition on the beach. Unfortunately, at this time of year, sailing isn't possible, due to the lack of wind.

We'll provide towels and beach chairs, but please <u>don't forget the sun-cream</u> as the temperatures are very high – you'll need it even on a cloudy day! The bus... (fade …)

Now listen again.

[repeat]

That is the end of Part Three.

PART 4　　*Now look at Part Four.*

For each question, choose the correct answer.

Look at questions 20 to 25 now. You have 45 seconds

You will hear an interview with a man called James Sweeney who works as a tree-climbing instructor.

Woman:　　I'm talking to James Sweeney, who's a tree-climbing instructor. He teaches people who want to learn for different reasons. How did you get interested in trees, James?

Man:　　I grew up around trees, because my mother was a garden designer. I often spent time in the gardens she worked on, although I wasn't allowed to go up the trees. What really got me into them was that <u>Mom had a friend</u> who was an arborist – someone who takes care of trees – and <u>he offered me a job one summer</u>.

Woman:　　And then you went on a course to learn to climb trees. How was that?

Man:　　Well <u>I was expecting everyone in the class to be young and fit</u>, because I thought you needed to be strong to climb trees. In fact <u>there were middle-aged climbers, children – even old people</u>! There was obviously special equipment to make climbing safe. We stayed in the trees for hours because it was so much fun!

Woman: And then you became a teacher of tree-climbing yourself … What do you enjoy most about it?

Man: It's great to be in the open, although not so much in the rain or when it's very hot. And I like working with people. Particularly <u>teaching those whose jobs involve having to go up trees</u>, like scientists, for example. There aren't so many of them – most people come because of happy memories of a childhood tree-climbing experience.

Woman: You often travel around the USA, too. Why?

Man: I live and work in the north-west of this country, and <u>no-one wants to climb trees there in the winter</u>. So I move around. I've climbed trees in every US state except Alaska! And in other countries – there's actually more interest in the subject abroad than here though.

Woman: And you like sleeping in trees, I understand. Why's that?

Man: <u>It's such a great place to get views of the night sky.</u> People say it must be uncomfortable, but you get used to it – it's not that bad really. You can't wake up late in the trees though – even a tiny bird sounds very loud when it's only a few inches from your head!

Woman: You've climbed trees in rainforests too. How is that different?

Man: The climbing's more challenging – not because the trees are harder to climb, but because you have to move more slowly. <u>It's an important environment, so you need to be careful not to damage it.</u> There are insects living in the trees too. If you go fast you attract them, and you're more likely to get bitten.

Woman: Thanks, James… (fade)

Now listen again.

[repeat]

That is the end of Part Four.

You now have six minutes to write your answers on the answer sheet.

You have one more minute.

That is the end of the test.

Test 4 answer key

Reading

Further feedback available in the downloadable resources

Part 1

1 C   **2** C   **3** B   **4** C   **5** A

Part 2

6 D   **7** H   **8** F   **9** B   **10** E

Part 3

11 C   **12** B   **13** A   **14** D   **15** B

Part 4

16 G   **17** B   **18** H   **19** E   **20** D

Part 5

21 B   **22** D   **23** A   **24** C   **25** A   **26** D

Part 6

27 since   **28** me   **29** for   **30** same   **31** one / some   **32** than

Writing

Question 1

Sample answer A

Hi Jo,

I want to thank you again for inviting me to come with you on this holiday. I would love to do some surfing and also to lie on the beach.
I am so sorry but I am not free in August because we have a lot of stress at work. What do you think if we go for a week in July? I have only one question about the holiday... Is everything inclusive or do we have to pay on our own for meals and stuff like this? I am so excited for the holiday with you.

See you soon! Caterina.

Subscale	Mark	Commentary
Content	5	All content is relevant to the task. The target reader is fully informed about all four points in the task.
Communicative Achievement	5	The email is written in a consistent register and a polite, friendly tone has been used, *Hi Jo*; *I want to thank you*; *I would love*; *I am so sorry*; *What do you think if*; *I am so excited*; *See you soon*. The email shows a range of functional language, including explanations, opinions and questions, which help to communicate straightforward ideas and hold the reader's attention.
Organisation	5	The text is well-organised and coherent at both sentence and text level. It follows the sequence of the input material, and the ideas are linked by the use of questions, which introduce the next idea, *What do you think*; *I have only one question*, and linking words, *and also*; *but*; *because*; *or*. The paragraphs are well balanced and the positive attitude is repeated through the text, *I want to thank you*; *I would love to*; *I am so excited*.
Language	5	The vocabulary is suitable for the task and there are some good collocations used appropriately, *thank you again*; *for inviting me*; *have a lot of stress*; *we go for a week*; *everything inclusive*; *meals and stuff like this*. The grammatical structures are used accurately and very naturally, and there are minimal errors, preposition slips, in the text, *pay on our own meals*; *so excited for*.

Sample answer B

> Hi Jo, how are you?
>
> I'm really *excited that we are going* together in holidays. Thanks, *that I can come with* you. It sounds really great. I love the beach. I'd like *do surfing and also lie on the beach* it's fantastic!
>
> I'd like *to go in the end of July*, because in August *I haven't got any* holidays I must work. Could *that be possible* for you? It would be nice.
>
> *Are we going alone?* *Or is coming someone else* with us? *Tell me as possible as you can.* *Hear you soon!*
>
> Morena

Subscale	Mark	Commentary
Content	5	All content is relevant to the task. The target reader is fully informed as all four points in the task have been covered.
Communicative Achievement	3	The email is written in an appropriate informal register, *Hi Jo*; *it sounds really great*; *I love*, and the tone is friendly and positive, *I'm really excited*; *it's fantastic*; *It would be nice*. The ideas are quite simple and there is some repetition from the input material, *Thanks that I can come with you*; *I'd like do surfing and also lie on the beach*, but the third point is developed quite well giving an alternative time to go and a reason why.
Organisation	3	The text is connected and coherent, following the structure of the input material. Some of the sentences are quite short, which limits the number of linking words used. However, the paragraphs are used well to focus on one idea at a time and there are some simple linking and referencing words, *It*; *and also*; *because*; *that*; *Or*. The layout of the email is very clear.
Language	3	There are some positive adjectives which are used appropriately for the task, *excited*; *great*; *fantastic*, but a lot of the vocabulary is repeated from the input material. The grammatical structures are quite simple, but generally accurate, *I'm really excited that we are going*; *I'd like to go in the end of July*; *I haven't got any*; *Could that be possible*; *Are we going alone?* There are some errors with particular phrases, either with word order or missing or wrong words, *I'd like do*; *Or is coming someone else*; *Tell me as possible as you can*; *Hear you soon*. However, the message can still be understood.

Question 2

Sample answer A

LEARNING LANGUAGES

I think it's very important to learn a foreign language because if you'll speak another language it's easier to talk in different country. Also if you're looking for a new job like travel agent etc. you have to know english language very well for example.

But on the other side it's really hard to learn them and so much harder if you're studying on your own. In group or with teacher you can practise it in conversations etc. but on your own you have only the internet or books. My advice is try to find people or teacher who will help you with learning foreign language.

Lucie Schlosserová

Subscale	Mark	Commentary
Content	5	All content is relevant to the task. The target reader is fully informed as all points in the task have been covered.
Communicative Achievement	5	The article has been written in an appropriately neutral register, suitable for a magazine. The article gives an opinion on why languages are important, *it's easier to talk in different country*; *new job like travel agent*, and presents a balanced view of the positives and negatives of the different ways to learn them, *In group or with teacher you can practise*; *on your own you only have the internet or books*. The reader's attention is held due to the objective tone of the article and the recommendation at the end, *My advice is*.
Organisation	5	The text is generally well-organised and the paragraphs are well structured, focusing on the separate questions in the task. The use of a heading provides a clear focus for the article. There is a variety of linking words and cohesive devices used to connect the ideas across the whole text, *because*; *if you'll speak…it's easier*; *Also*; *for example*; *But on the other side it's really hard…and so much harder*; *In group…but on your own*; *who*.
Language	5	There is a range of vocabulary used appropriately, *different country*; *new job*; *travel agent*; *conversations*; *internet*; *advice*. There is a range of grammatical structures, including conditionals, used with accuracy, *if you're looking…you have to know*. Comparative structures are used effectively as well, *it's really hard to learn them and so much harder*; *In group or with teacher…but on your own*. There are minor errors, some of which are possibly slips, *if you'll speak*; *or teacher*.

136

Sample answer B

> In my opinion is really important to learn a foreign languages, because than you will understand in foreign states, when you for example will go on holidays. And this is true: "It's better to know more than you can learn in school"
>
> I think it's different for everybody. Somebody can like study in a group and another one on his/her own. But for me it's better to learn a language in a group because I can discutating about it with the others and learn alot of from them or from the teacher. When you study alone, you have to find all information on your own a there is noto anybody who can helps you.

Subscale	Mark	Commentary
Content	5	All content is relevant to the task. The target reader is fully informed as all questions in the task have been covered.
Communicative Achievement	4	The article is written in a semi-formal register and both general and personal views are given, *you will understand*; *when you for example will go on holidays*; *But for me it's better*; *When you study alone.* The topic is clearly introduced and there is language of opinion and explanation throughout the text which communicates straightforward ideas to the reader.
Organisation	3	The text is simply organised into paragraphs and each one focuses on one of the aspects in the task. There is some use of linking words, *because*; *when*; *And*; *But*, and simple cohesive devices are used to introduce and connect the ideas through the text, *In my opinion*; *for example*; *Somebody…and another one*; *the others*; *them*; *who*. These cohesive devices make it clear to the reader whose opinions or preferences are being described.
Language	3	The vocabulary is suitable for the task and it is used generally appropriately, *states*; *holidays*; *teacher*; *information*, although there are some errors, *discutating*. The structures are quite simple, but accurate, generally using the present tense or simple forms of the future, *will understand*; *will go*; *better to know more than you can learn*; *learn alot from them*; *When you study alone, you have to find*. There are some errors, but these do not affect communication, *can like study*; *a there is noto anybody who can helps you*.

Question 3

Sample answer A

> The friends got off the bus and ran over to join the long queue of people. I then realised J.K. Rowling was signing books for people. Of course, I joined them. After one hour which felt like one decade, it was my turn.
>
> I handed her the book which always been inside my bag and she signed it. She asked my name and I told her. I'm pretty sure that my voice was shaking but she was so kind and acting nothing happened. I told her that I have been a fan of her and requested a picture with her.
>
> After I'm done, I joined my friends. I think I shrieked a little but overall, it was a great experience.

Subscale	Mark	Commentary
Content	5	All content is relevant to the task. The target reader is fully informed as the story follows on logically from the prompt sentence.
Communicative Achievement	4	Although the prompt focuses on a group of friends getting off the bus, the story continues in the first person and it is not immediately clear what the relationship is between the friends, the queue and the narrator. However, the story has a clear sequence of events and other features of a narrative, including reported speech and description, are included, *After one hour which felt like one decade*; *She asked my name and I told her*; *I told her that*. The events are clearly described and there is an obvious sense of excitement.
Organisation	5	The story is generally well-organised and uses some cohesive devices to show the order of events, *then*; *After one hour*; *After I'm done*. There is a variety of linking words used to connect the ideas within sentences, *which*; *and*; *but*; *overall*, and there is a clear beginning, middle and an end, *it was a great experience*.
Language	5	There is a range of vocabulary, which is appropriate for the task and which describes how special the event was, *realised*; *signing books*; *decade*; *pretty sure*; *shaking*; *kind*; *fan*; *requested*; *shrieked*. There is good control of past tenses, both simple and continuous forms, *I then realised J.K. Rowling was signing books*; *my voice was shaking, but she was so kind*. There are some minor slips of control, *which always been inside*; *I have been a fan of her*; *After I'm done*, but these do not affect how well the message has been communicated.

Sample answer B

The friends got off the bus and ran over to join the long queue of people. The company with the name "pineaplle" has presented the new fascion smartpfone with 7 cameras and 2 screens. All of the people wanted to buy thir phone. Some of them were ready to stay in the queue for 6 hours to buy it. And that's crazy! Our friends joined the queue. It was realy big. About 20 meters long. Our friend Alex is really funny. Sudenly he fell down on the woman that stayed forward. And all of the people started to fell like dominos. All of the people laughed. That was fun.

Subscale	Mark	Commentary
Content	5	All content is relevant to the task. The target reader is fully informed as the story follows on logically from the prompt sentence.
Communicative Achievement	3	The story is quite straightforward with some description of what the people are queueing for and why this is exciting, *has presented the new fascion smartpfone*; *people wanted to buy thir phone*. There is also an event described when the friends join the queue, *Sudenly he fell down on the woman…And all of the people started to fell like dominos*. The story is told in a series of quite short sentences which limits the overall effectiveness of the story.
Organisation	3	The story has a clear overall structure but the individual aspects are not always connected effectively, *And that's crazy! Our friends joined the queue. It was realy big; About 20 metres long. Our friend Alex is really funny*. More use of linking words between these sentences would make the story more cohesive. However, there are a few examples of cohesive devices being used, such as relative pronouns to avoid repetition, *thir phone*; *Some of them*.
Language	3	The vocabulary is appropriate for the task, *company*; *crazy*; *fell down*; *dominos*; *laughed*. There is some accurate use of tenses and other grammatical structures, *All of the people wanted to buy*; *were ready to stay in the queue for 6 hours to buy it*, and even when there are errors with grammatical forms, the meaning is still clear, *has presented*; *And all of the people started to fell like dominos*. There are some errors with spelling, but these do not impede communication, *fascion*; *smartpfone*; *thir*; *realy*.

Test 4 answer key

Listening

Part 1

1 B   **2** A   **3** A   **4** C   **5** C   **6** A   **7** B

Part 2

8 A   **9** C   **10** A   **11** C   **12** A   **13** A

Part 3

14 five / 5   **15** bikes / bicycles   **16** lake   **17** butterflies
18 castle   **19** bus (service)

Part 4

20 A   **21** C   **22** B   **23** A   **24** B   **25** C

Further feedback available in the downloadable resources

Transcript

Test Four. There are four parts to the test. You will hear each part twice. We will now stop for a moment. Please ask any questions now, because you must not speak during the test.

PART 1   *Now look at the instructions for Part One*

For each question, choose the correct answer. Look at question one.

Question 1   *One. How will the man travel to the city centre?*

Man: Excuse me, what's the best way to get to the city centre?

Woman: Well, it's probably easiest to take a taxi, especially if you've got a lot of luggage.

Man: I've just got a light bag. Is there a bus that goes there?

Woman: Yes there is, but it takes quite a long route. <u>What about the underground?</u> It's a short walk from here and the trains go every 10 minutes. It'd be faster than a taxi.

Man: <u>That sounds perfect. I'll do that.</u> Thanks so much for your help.

Woman: No problem.

Now listen again.

[repeat]

Question 2   *Two. What did the girl dislike at the hostel she stayed in?*

Man: How was your holiday?

Girl: Good. The hostel was ok but not great!

Man: Oh, I've heard about problems with mice in some of the hostels in the area you visited.

Girl: Really? Well, they've obviously done something about that. <u>The thing was, our beds didn't have mosquito nets, so we got bitten almost every night.</u> Even after putting on insect cream.

Man: Right.

Girl: And then every morning we heard monkeys running across the roof, I didn't mind that at all though – it was like being in a hostel in the jungle!

Now listen again.

[repeat]

Question 3   *Three. What is the man going to order for lunch?*

Woman: What are you going to order, then?

Man: Let me see. (slight pause) I think I'd like the salmon.

Woman: You're so boring! I knew you'd say fish! You never try anything different. I'm having pizza – they make them really thin and tasty here.

Man: Yes, my sister had one last time we ate here – she said it was great!

Woman: How about the curry? That's excellent, I believe.

Man: Mmm. Nice idea, but I've heard it's very spicy. I've made up my mind. I'll have what I always have!

Woman: (laughs) Of course!

Now listen again.

[repeat]

Question 4   *Four. What sport would the woman like to try?*

Woman: I've decided to take up a new sport. There are lots of classes starting at the sports centre near the golf course.

Man: What sport are you thinking of doing?

Woman: Well, I did consider golf. When I looked at the cost though, I realised it's way more than I can afford. Anyway, I'm not that good at racket sports but I wouldn't mind giving badminton a go. You need to be so strong to play tennis.

Man: I might do a new sports class too.

Woman: Hey! Come along with me.

Now listen again.

[repeat]

Question 5   *Five. Which book is the man reading?*

Woman: What's the book you're reading about?

Man: It's a novel by one of my favourite writers. A lot of his books are based on his experiences flying planes around the world. This one's set at sea – a guy who crosses the Pacific Ocean on his own and all the challenges he has to deal with. I've heard he's working on a new one at the moment about an astronaut, who goes to the moon and can't get back. It sounds interesting. Anyway, this one's really exciting.

Woman: Sounds cool.

Now listen again.

[repeat]

Question 6   *Six. Where does the man suggest going at the weekend?*

Man: Hi Sue. It's Matt. Thanks for your message. I think it's a great idea to go out for the day at the weekend. You mentioned going for a walk on the beach. I've just looked at the weather forecast though and there might be a storm coming. There's a new art exhibition on at the museum – definitely worth seeing, or so I've heard. I wondered about going to the cinema, and had a look at what's on. There's nothing very exciting this weekend. Anyway, let me know what you think. Bye!

Now listen again.

[repeat]

Question 7 *Seven. How much is the latest smartphone in the store today?*

Man: At ABC's phone store, we've got some fantastic offers this week. <u>For an amazing £599, the most up-to-date smartphone is now available</u>. It's got a great camera and the biggest memory ever. But hurry, this offer is only on for a few days. If you wait till Monday, it'll be back to its usual price of £699. If either of these prices is more than you can afford, there's always last year's model which is just £499. But don't delay, when they're gone, they're gone. Come early to avoid disappointment.

Now listen again.

[repeat]

That is the end of Part One.

PART 2 *Now look at Part Two. For each question, choose the correct answer.*

Question 8 *Eight. You will hear a brother and sister talking about a gift for their cousin.*

Man: So what do you think we should give our cousin Lucy for her birthday? She's just moved into her new apartment.

Woman: I think she'd like a microwave. In fact, I've already had a quick look online and seen a few special offers.

Man: Shall we go and have a look in the big department store in town?

Woman: What for? It's likely to be more expensive. And besides, <u>it weighs so much, can you imagine us trying to take it on the bus?</u>

Man: OK, but we'd better hurry up and order online, or they might not have any left.

Now listen again.

[repeat]

Question 9 *Nine. You will hear two colleagues discussing their holiday travel plans.*

Woman: I've finally decided on my holiday plans. What about you?

Man: Well, actually, I'm going to Greece next week. And you?

Woman: We're off to the coast of Ireland in a month's time.

Man: <u>Going by car and the ferry again?</u>

Woman: Yes.

Man: You must love it – you go there every holiday!

Woman: I do. And this time we're going for a fortnight, not just a week. So that's exciting.

Man: <u>Wouldn't it be better if you flew?</u> You wouldn't waste so much time getting to where you're going.

Woman: We like to be able to get around easily once we're there.

Now listen again.

[repeat]

Question 10 *Ten. You will hear a man talking to a friend about a fitness training session.*

Man: Hi Joanna. I'm afraid I can't make today's fitness training session.

Woman: Oh? Are you OK?

Man: Well, I'm not too bad. I had this really awful cold, which took about a week to get rid of. Fortunately it's over now. <u>But my doctor told me to take things easy anyway</u> – I don't know if I mentioned it to you – I need to have an operation on my foot on Friday. It's nothing serious, though. I'll be back at fitness training very soon.

Woman: Oh good! Well, you take care then. See you.

Man: Okay, but we'd better hurry up and order online, or they might not have any left.

Now listen again.

[repeat]

Question 11 *Eleven. You will hear two friends talking about a play they've just seen.*

Man: That play was really great, wasn't it?

Woman: I thought the second half was a bit less interesting than the first. You could predict exactly what was going to happen.

Man: Really? I wasn't sure how it would end. The actors were excellent though, weren't they?

Woman: Well actually I expected the performances to be a lot better. I must say though the costumes were brilliant.

Man: I think you're a bit hard to please when you go to the theatre, so why don't you choose the next play we see?

Woman: OK, well, I hope you'll like what I choose!

Now listen again.

[repeat]

Question 12 *Twelve. You will hear two friends talking about a film and its soundtrack.*

Man: What are you listening to on your phone?

Woman: The soundtrack to that film, Smash. Have you seen it?

Man: Not yet.

Woman: I've got it – we could watch it together. It'd be a nice thing to do after a hard week of work.

Man: Cool. I'm free on Friday.

Woman: I mean, the film's aimed at kids, but I think you'll like it. The music's definitely popular with a much wider range of people. Some of it's good old-fashioned jazz and soul, but it's got a sound that makes you want to get up and move. It's definitely as good as the film.

Now listen again.

[repeat]

Question 13 *Thirteen. You will hear two friends talking about the news.*

Man: Why are you always looking at your laptop?

Woman: I'm checking what's happening in the world. I make sure I do it every morning before anything else.

Man: So do I. I need to for my job. But I much prefer reading a real newspaper.

Woman: But online I can focus on what I'm really interested in, rather than all the stuff about celebrities and sport stars. I just don't care.

Man: There's a lot of that, but I must admit I always enjoy reading about their lives.

Woman: Do you? Well, there's actually more about that sort of thing online.

Now listen again.

[repeat]

That is the end of Part Two.

PART 3   *Now look at Part Three.*

For each question, write the correct answer in the gap. Write one or two words or a number or a date or a time. Look at questions 14 to 19 now. You have 20 seconds.

You will hear a guide giving some information about a walk in the countryside.

Man: Welcome, everyone. I'm Mike, your guide on today's walk in the beautiful countryside here.

I'm sure you'll want to know how long the walk will take. Well, there are two possible routes, <u>one of which takes four hours, and the other five. We'll be taking the longer one, as it has fewer hills.</u> We'll be at our destination by around two.

Right, things to be careful of. It's a fairly easy route, and there are good paths. There are some steps to climb in some parts, but in this dry weather you won't slip. <u>Please look out for bikes, though.</u> Cars aren't a problem, as our route avoids public roads.

I hope you've all remembered to bring lunch with you, as the café at the visitor centre we'll pass is closed for repairs. Instead, I've picked <u>a great place to eat by the lake.</u> We'll also have a shorter break at the waterfall, so you can take photos.

For people who are interested in wildlife, there's plenty to see. You'll be pleased to know that <u>there are lots of butterflies at this time of year.</u> The forest is famous for its frogs, but they stay hidden away during the daytime unfortunately.

<u>At the end of our walk,</u> I'm afraid you won't find a shop selling souvenirs, or anything like that. <u>There is a castle,</u> though. It's not very big, but it is interesting, and a nice place to rest after a long walk!

Finally you'll want to get back to where we started! There used to be a railway station in the area, but it's been many years since a train went through there. <u>There's a bus service,</u> although you may have to wait a while. A taxi driver will never come this far out of town, so that's really the only option.

Right, let's go!

Now listen again.

[repeat]

That is the end of Part Three.

PART 4   *Now look at Part Four.*

For each question, choose the correct answer. Look at questions 20 to 25 now. You have 45 seconds.

You will hear an interview with a young poet called Laura Dickson.

Presenter: Laura Dickson, you've already had two books of your poems published. How did you become interested in poetry?

Laura: Well, my dad loves literature so there were always <u>lots of poetry books on the shelves around the house. I used to spend hours looking at them</u>. I'm pleased it happened that way, because there needs to be more time spent on it at school. I think students would enjoy it.

Presenter: And how did you decide to turn your interest into a career as a professional poet?

Laura: I started doing some classes in journalism. I showed my poems to the woman running the course. She was a well-known reporter on a national newspaper, and she suggested that <u>I enter a poetry competition. I did, and two months later found out I'd come first</u>. That's when I knew I wanted to do this full-time.

Presenter: So, I hear you've just finished a new book of poems. What's it about?

Laura: You never exactly know what poems are going to be about until you start writing them, and my previous books have included my thoughts about architecture – ancient and new. In this one, though, <u>I focus on connections with the people I'm close to</u>. I actually started out with the idea of writing about global warming and the environment, which is very different to what I produced in the end.

Presenter: Your poetry's very modern. Do you read poetry written a long time ago?

Laura: Yes, I do. The words and style are often very different from modern English. <u>But you soon notice how carefully the poems have been put together. I think they took more skill to write than many modern ones do.</u>

Presenter: And you've also started teaching poetry at a university recently. How's that going?

Laura: I'm certainly enjoying it, even if I'm not always sure how much my students are actually learning. <u>Thankfully the other teachers have a lot more experience than me and are happy to share their ideas.</u> I was warned about how much preparation there'd be, so that wasn't too much of a shock.

Presenter: And what are your plans for the future?

Laura: Well, there's a poetry festival soon, and the organisers have asked me to read my work at it. <u>I'm hoping to turn some of my previous work into songs</u> – after all, hip-hop and rap are just poetry with a tune. New poems come into my head all the time too – I'd get worried if I had to stop writing because I'd run out of ideas.

Presenter: Thank you, Laura…. (fade)

Now listen again.

[repeat]

That is the end of Part Four.

You now have six minutes to write your answers on the answer sheet.

You have one more minute.

That is the end of the test.

Sample answer sheet: Reading

Draft

Cambridge Assessment
English

Candidate Name		Candidate Number	
Centre Name		Centre Number	
Examination Title		Examination Details	
Candidate Signature		Assessment Date	

Supervisor: If the candidate is ABSENT or has WITHDRAWN shade here ○

Preliminary Reading Candidate Answer Sheet

Instructions
Use a PENCIL (B or HB)
Rub out any answer you want to change with an eraser.

For Parts 1, 2, 3, 4 and 5:
Mark ONE letter for each answer.
For example: If you think A is the right answer to
the question, mark your answer sheet like this:

Part 1

	A	B	C
1	○	○	○
2	○	○	○
3	○	○	○
4	○	○	○
5	○	○	○

Part 2

	A	B	C	D	E	F	G	H
6	○	○	○	○	○	○	○	○
7	○	○	○	○	○	○	○	○
8	○	○	○	○	○	○	○	○
9	○	○	○	○	○	○	○	○
10	○	○	○	○	○	○	○	○

Part 3

	A	B	C	D
11	○	○	○	○
12	○	○	○	○
13	○	○	○	○
14	○	○	○	○
15	○	○	○	○

Part 4

	A	B	C	D	E	F	G	H
16	○	○	○	○	○	○	○	○
17	○	○	○	○	○	○	○	○
18	○	○	○	○	○	○	○	○
19	○	○	○	○	○	○	○	○
20	○	○	○	○	○	○	○	○

Part 5

	A	B	C	D
21	○	○	○	○
22	○	○	○	○
23	○	○	○	○
24	○	○	○	○
25	○	○	○	○
26	○	○	○	○

Continues over ➡

Draft

Draft

For Part 6:
Write your answers clearly in the spaces next to the numbers (27 to 32) like this:

| 0 | E N G L I S H |

Write your answers in CAPITAL LETTERS.

Part 6	Do not write below here
27	27 1 0 ○ ○
28	28 1 0 ○ ○
29	29 1 0 ○ ○
30	30 1 0 ○ ○
31	31 1 0 ○ ○
32	32 1 0 ○ ○

Draft

You must write within the grey lines.

Write your answer for Part 1 below. Do not write on the barcodes.

Question 1

This section for use by Examiner only:

C	CA	O	L

* 0010437500302 *

© UCLES 2019   Photocopiable

You must write within the grey lines.

Answer only one of the two questions for Part 2.
Tick the box to show which question you have answered.
Write your answer below. Do not write on the barcodes.

Part 2	Question 2		Question 3	

This section for use by Examiner only:

C	CA	O	L

* 0010437500303 *

Sample answer sheet: Listening

Draft

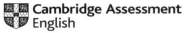 **Cambridge Assessment**
English

Candidate Name		Candidate Number	
Centre Name		Centre Number	
Examination Title		Examination Details	
Candidate Signature		Assessment Date	

Supervisor: If the candidate is ABSENT or has WITHDRAWN shade here ○

Preliminary Listening Candidate Answer Sheet

Instructions
Use a PENCIL (B or HB). Rub out any answer you want to change with an eraser.

For Parts 1, 2 and 4:
Mark one letter for each answer. For example: If you think **A** is the right answer to the question, mark your answer sheet like this:

For Part 3:
Write your answers clearly in the spaces next to the numbers (14 to 19) like this:

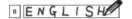

Write your answers in CAPITAL LETTERS.

Part 1

	A	B	C
1	○	○	○
2	○	○	○
3	○	○	○
4	○	○	○
5	○	○	○
6	○	○	○
7	○	○	○

Part 2

	A	B	C
8	○	○	○
9	○	○	○
10	○	○	○
11	○	○	○
12	○	○	○
13	○	○	○

Part 3

		Do not write below here
14		14 1 ○ 0 ○
15		15 1 ○ 0 ○
16		16 1 ○ 0 ○
17		17 1 ○ 0 ○
18		18 1 ○ 0 ○
19		19 1 ○ 0 ○

Part 4

	A	B	C
20	○	○	○
21	○	○	○
22	○	○	○
23	○	○	○
24	○	○	○
25	○	○	○

Draft

Acknowledgements

The authors and publishers acknowledge the following sources of copyright material and are grateful for the permissions granted. While every effort has been made, it has not always been possible to identify the sources of all the material used, or to trace all copyright holders. If any omissions are brought to our notice, we will be happy to include the appropriate acknowledgements on reprinting and in the next update to the digital edition, as applicable.

Photographs

Key: T = Test, R = Reading, ST = Speaking Test, P = Part.

All the photographs are sourced from Getty Images.

T1 R P2: Granger Wootz/Blend Images; Javier Sánchez Mingorance / EyeEm; Flashpop/DigitalVision; Indeed; rubberball; **T2 R P2:** LeoPatrizi/iStock/Getty Images Plus; Jason Todd/The Image Bank; Westend61; Compassionate Eye Foundation/DigitalVision; Calvin Dolley/Photographer's Choice; **T3 R P2:** Easy Production/ Cultura; BLOOMimage; theboone/E+; Gregory Costanzo/DigitalVision; Lena Koller/Johner Images; **T4 R P2:** Peter Widmann/ EyeEm; Juanmonino/E+; Klaus Vedfelt/Taxi; AntonioGuillem/iStock/Getty Images Plus; Kay Fochtmann/EyeEm; **T1 ST:** Hero Images; Eugenio Marongiu/Cultura; **T2 ST:** Maskot; Pat Canova/Photolibrary; **T3 ST:** Astronaut Images/Caiaimage; Hero Images; **T4 ST:** BJI/Lane Oatey; SolStock/E+.

Typeset by QBS Learning.

Audio production by Real Deal Productions and dsound recording Ltd.

Visual materials for the Speaking test

Test 1

Part 2

Task 1A

Task 1B

Test 1

Part 3

Task 1C

Choosing a book about interesting people

Test 2

Part 2

Task 2A

Task 2B

Test 2

Part 3

Task 2C

A present to take to a cold country

Test 3

Part 2

Task 3A

Task 3B

Test 3

Part 3

Task 3C

Using an empty building

Test 4

Part 2

Task 4A

Task 4B

Test 4

Part 3

Task 4C

Helping the environment

SPOT THE DIFFERENCE

That's right – there is no difference.

All our authentic practice tests go through the same design process as the official exam. We check every single part of our practice tests with real students under exam conditions, to make sure we give you the most authentic experience possible.

The official practice tests from Cambridge.